BATTLE

MW00532392

KING'S MOUNTAIN

BATTLEGROUND AMERICA GUIDES offer a unique approach to the battles and battlefields of America. Each book in the series highlights a small American battlefield—sometimes a small portion of a much larger battlefield. All of the units, important individuals, and actions of each engagement on the battlefield are described in a clear and concise narrative. Historical images and modern-day photographs tie the dramatic events of the past to today's battlefield site and highlight the importance of terrain in battle. The present-day battlefield is described in detail with suggestions for touring the site.

KING'S MOUNTAIN

The Defeat of the Loyalists, October 7, 1780

J. David Dameron

DA CAPO PRESS
A Member of the Perseus Books Group

For my parents,
Jerry and Jean Dameron

Copyright © 2003 by Da Capo Press

Cataloging-in-Publication data for this book is
available from the Library of Congress.
ISBN 0-306-81194-4

Published by Da Capo Press
A Member of the Perseus Books Group
http://www.dacapopress.com

Da Capo Press books are available at special discounts for bulk
purchases in the U.S. by corporations, institutions, and other
organizations. For more information, please contact the Special
Markets Department at the Perseus Books Group, 11 Cambridge
Center, Cambridge, MA 02142, or call (617) 252-5298.

1 2 3 4 5 6 7 8 9—05 04 03

CONTENTS

PREFACE

I FIRST LEARNED ABOUT THE Battle of King's Mountain as a boy. Since I grew up in the South, the picnics and mock battles (my sisters were always the enemy) I enjoyed at battlefield parks are cherished childhood memories. I was attracted to the romance of the American Revolution, and I even persuaded my parents to buy me a felt trihorn hat and a toy flintlock pistol. I was "king of the mountain" for months thereafter, until the enemy (my sisters) crushed my hat and hid my pistol. While the Battle of King's Mountain was briefly mentioned in my high school history class, I remember my confusion concerning the 1,000 "British Redcoats" that were defeated by the Patriots in their "blue uniforms." Yet, the dramatic story of King's Mountain never left me, I read all the accounts that I could on the subject, and I learned on my own what really happened at this battle. While the Bicentennial celebrations of 1976 brought a renewed interest in the Revolutionary War, and especially to King's Mountain, since then, interest in the Revolution has generally waned. While studying history in college, I discovered that several of my ancestors served in the Patriot militia, but I also learned that the ancestors of a close friend served in the Loyalist militia. While both our southern families were of English heritage, during the American Revolution, our ancestors would have hated one another. Years later, while serving in the military, I learned the intimate details concerning the brutal nature of partisan warfare and revolutions. Thus, my personal interest in the

Battle of King's Mountain runs very deeply and its relevance is profoundly important to the histories of both the United States and Great Britain.

A popular movie entitled *The Patriot* has created a renewed interest in the Revolutionary War. By highlighting the Patriots' struggle in the Carolinas, the movie gives us a glimpse of the emotional drama and violent rage that swept through our nation. While its fictional account of affairs is only loosely based on actual history, I hope the movie will encourage families to visit our battlefield parks. It is my earnest desire that this book will serve as your guide in comprehending the events that transpired on King's Mountain. The mountain, its monuments, its graves, and the spirit of the Revolution await you.

J. David Dameron
March 2003

INTRODUCTION

THE BATTLE OF KING'S MOUNTAIN, waged on October 7, 1780, was a significant victory for the American colonies. It was a turning point in the American Revolution and a great morale booster—a band of partisans totally decimated the entire left wing of a seemingly invincible British Army. Stunned by the staggering defeat, Lord Cornwallis ordered his invading army to retreat, and his campaign to conquer the Carolinas was delayed for many months. The battle struck a fatal blow to the Loyalist movement in America and the victory provided the Patriots valuable time to rebuild their army. The battle, in which unconventional forces soundly defeated traditional European troops, also signaled a change in military thinking. The Americans used flexible infantry maneuver, cover and concealment, and rifles, while their British-led adversaries employed massed formations, bayonet assaults, and muskets.

Moreover, this battle was waged by men whose courage and tenacity serves as a source of pride for all posterity. Except for the British commander, all of the men in this battle were Americans, and it is this mysterious fact that frequently lures curiosity. While the American Patriots fought British Redcoats in the open field of battle, they waged a much darker war against their own neighbors, the Loyalist Militia.

VIRGINIA
TENN.
Sycamore Shoals
Hillsborough
Guilford Courthouse
Catawba
Quaker Meadows
NORTH CAROLINA
Broad
Gilbert Town
Charlotte
King's Mountain
Cowpens
Broad
Waxhaws
Cape Fear
Pee Dee
Camden
Saluda
Ninety Six
Savannah
SOUTH CAROLINA
GEORGIA
Atlantic Ocean
Charleston
0
50 Miles

1

THE ROAD TO KING'S MOUNTAIN

BEFORE THE LATTER PART OF 1779, the bulk of the American Revolution had been waged in and around New England. In the south, the British had held the port city of Savannah for nearly a year, and the Americans were unable to repulse them. Warships of the French Navy attempted to help the Americans, but the British fleet dominated the coast and the French retreated to the West Indies. The commander of the British forces, Sir Henry Clinton (1730–1795) was ordered by King George III (1738–1820) to crush the rebellion in the Southern Theater and then press northward. With a maritime force of 13,000 men and 100 ships, the British sailed to the south on December 26, 1779. Clinton personally led his invasion force into the harbor of Charleston, South Carolina. The patriot defenders could not withstand the resulting siege and on May 12, 1780, General Benjamin Lincoln (1733–1810) surrendered his forces to the British invaders.

When Charleston fell, the Loyalist sympathizers in South Carolina rallied to the aid of the British army. An integral part of Clinton's plan was to capitalize on these resources, regain South Carolina's complete allegiance to the Crown, and conquer the entire Southern province. In fact, Clinton stated that his campaign would meet with success as long as "the temper of our friends in those districts is such as it has always been represented to us." Once South Carolina

Lord Earl Cornwallis

was secure, he could then roll his military machine into North Carolina and on into Virginia. The coastal environs were rapidly conquered and the British established outposts along a northwest corridor deep into South Carolina.

With his army making headway in the Southern Campaign, Clinton appointed Lord Charles Earl Cornwallis (1738–1805) as the commander of his Southern forces, and then he returned to the Northern Theater to counter the arrival of the Marquis de Lafayette (1757–1834) and the French. The British army strengthened its grip on South Carolina and Cornwallis sent promises of British assistance to Loyalist leaders in North Carolina. He then established his headquarters at Camden, South Carolina, and his command of 4,000 regular troops and provincial forces was bolstered greatly through local recruiting. The ranks of the Loyalist militia in South Carolina were robust. Reassured by the overwhelming strength of the British army, these Loyalists militiamen eagerly served the Crown.

No Briton was better in the art of recruiting Tories than Major Patrick Ferguson of the Seventy-first Regiment of Foot. He entered communities stating, "We come not to

make war on women and children, but to relieve their dis-
tresses." Ferguson knew these were powerful words for a
terrified people. He offered them security and stability; all
he wanted in return was loyalty and service. In the western
frontier district of Ninety-Six, Ferguson recruited and
formed seven battalions of militia, (nearly 4,000 men)
which were so well organized they included a 1,500-man
mobile reaction unit. Clinton personally appointed
Ferguson to the post of inspector general of militia forces,
and his militia or "territorial" rank was that of brigadier
general. By 1779 Ferguson had won a temporary appointment to the rank of lieutenant colonel. However, with his
assignment to head the militia, his official British rank
reverted to his full commission as a major. (The matter of
Ferguson's rank has been misstated in several historical
narratives; thus it is mentioned herein for clarification.)

Several of Ferguson's peers snubbed him because of his
achievements and his obvious favor with the commander-
in-chief, and they readily pointed out that Ferguson's
"command" was comprised of militia, not professional soldiers. Yet, Ferguson's work with the militia was critical to
the British army and Clinton had appointed the right man
to the task at hand. Ferguson was thirty-five years old
when charged with the responsibility of training, equip-
ping, organizing, and leading the Loyalist militia in battle,
and he was fully suited to the art of command. He wielded
a large silver whistle to control his forces, and through
incessant drilling, Ferguson's corps of Loyalist militia
became an army. Moreover, Ferguson had always championed the concept of the citizen-soldier and Clinton provided him the authority and opportunity to prove it.

Patrick Ferguson (1744–1780), the son of James and Anne
Ferguson, was born in Pitfours, Aberdeenshire, Scotland.
His family was well-educated, affluent, and highly
respected. His father was a judge and a nobleman. His
mother was a refined lady and the daughter of Alexander
Murray, fourth Lord Elibank. Her brother, British General

James Murray (1721–1794) arranged for young "Pattie" to attend the military academy in London, where he excelled in military science. Commenting on young Pattie's progress, General Murray once stated, "I mean to push him in my own profession," and he did. At the age of fifteen, his family purchased a commission for Pattie and he entered the king's service as a cornet in the Royal North British Dragoons, also known as the "Scott Greys." At the age of sixteen, while serving in the Seven Years' War against France, Ferguson was honored for "prodigies of valor."

From 1762 through 1768, Ferguson remained in Great Britain, where he grew into manhood. Throughout his life he suffered from several disabling maladies, but these were most likely the results of arduous military service and poor medical treatment. Physically, Ferguson was handsome, slender, and of average height. While he was well liked by the ladies, he never married. Military matters dominated his life and his friends referred to him as brilliant, intense, and talented. Within his letters his words reflect a well-educated and pensive man, and through his lifelong devotion to the military, despite his disabilities, he was apparently blessed with an indomitable spirit. During his six-year stay at home, Ferguson championed the organization and inclusion of local militias in the armed forces. The military establishment despised militias and merely tolerated their presence. Yet, Ferguson saw merit in the concept of the citizen-soldier and his work in this arena played a great role in his life.

From 1768 through 1773, he served as a captain in the Seventieth Regiment of Foot. His unit was dispatched to the Caribbean, where Ferguson led men in battle against uprisings in Tobago and St. Vincent. After a brief assignment in Nova Scotia, Ferguson returned to Great Britain, where he studied ordnance, designed and received a patent for a rifle bearing his name, and earned a reputation as the best shot in the British army. His prowess with arms is well-founded in history and even King George witnessed a

Major Patrick Ferguson; portrait by Robert Wilson

display of Ferguson's abilities. Ferguson was skilled with all the weapons of war, but with his "Ferguson Rifle" he could fire accurately from the prone position, and rapidly, which was unheard of in the eighteenth century. In fact his rifle was a breechloader, revolutionary in design, and its capabilities presented the military the possibility of modernizing tactics and doctrine. Ironically, the rifle's unusualness and the possibilities of changing military conventions probably doomed it from immediate adoption as the standard weapon of the British army. Besides, the English "Brown Bess" musket was battle-proven, popular, and had been the army's standard firearm since 1702.

In the meantime, the colonists in America revolted and Great Britain called for volunteers. Ferguson was anxious to participate and in 1777 he was selected to command a special 100-man unit. This unit was to be armed with the Ferguson Rifle and attached to General William Howe (1729–1814). At the Battle of Brandywine, "the Rifle Corps" commanded by Ferguson was later recognized for "gallant and spirited behavior." His unit and his rifle performed brilliantly, but Ferguson's right arm was shattered by a Patriot's bullet. His wound was serious and it removed him from command. In Ferguson's absence, his unit was disbanded and the Ferguson rifle fell into obscurity. While Ferguson's arm was saved from amputation, he never regained its use and during the next year, he learned to shoot and wield a sword with his left arm. Within a year, Ferguson was back in action, and he led several successful operations.

Sir Henry Clinton took note of Ferguson's contributions and attributed the success of one mission to "that very active and zealous officer, Ferguson." In October 1779, Ferguson was promoted to the rank of major in the Second Battalion, Seventy-first Regiment of Foot. This unit was an integral part of the Highland Light Infantry, a unit filled with proud Scotsmen and a valorous history. In December 1779, Clinton personally selected Ferguson to command a special unit known as the "American Volunteers," which was comprised of New York and New Jersey provincials. These men were Americans who remained loyal to Great Britain and served as professional soldiers. Most of them had seen combat in the Northern theater of war, their loyalty and professionalism was unquestioned, and they wore their British red coats with pride. Ferguson's command also included several hundred Hessians and his beloved Seventy-first Regiment of Foot. For this special assignment, Clinton brevetted Ferguson with the temporary rank of lieutenant colonel and gave him a unique opportunity to lead men into battle.

As the British fleet sailed southward it was blown off course by powerful storms. The harrowing journey finally delivered the fleet to southern shores, but much further south than desired. After a brief respite in Savannah, Georgia, the British fleet sailed for Charleston, South Carolina, where the soldiers would begin their invasion with a siege of the port city. First, however, Clinton decided to dispatch a land force northward to Charleston from Savannah. Its mission was to clear the sector between the

British "Brown Bess" .75 caliber musket, the
standard Infantry firearm of the American Revolution.

British "Brown Bess" .75 caliber musket

two coastal cities of rebel forces. Among the units Clinton selected for this task was Ferguson's corps. Lieutenant Colonel Ferguson found himself working with Lt. Col. Banastre Tarleton (1754–1833), whose dragoons were renowned for their rapid and aggressive operations. During a hazardous night operation, mistaken identities resulted in a brief accidental clash between the units of Ferguson and Tarleton. While the error was rapidly corrected, several men were killed and Ferguson's left arm—his only remaining good arm—was horribly slashed and mangled by a bayonet. It first appeared that Ferguson's arm would require amputation, but the determined warrior kept the infection in check and saved his arm. Within four days, Ferguson was literally back in the saddle, frequently with the reins in his teeth, and busy serving the Crown.

Ferguson and Tarleton continued their joint operations, but during their early days around Charleston, Ferguson learned to despise Tarleton. The two men were both devoutly loyal to king and country, but that is where their similarities end. Tarleton was a violent opportunist and he took pleasure in waging brutal, merciless combat. After the war he remarked that during the revolution, he had "killed more men and ravished more women than anyone in America." Ferguson was a professional soldier and he argued that Tarleton's men should be severely punished for their wanton "scorched-earth" techniques. On several occasions Ferguson called for an end to Tarleton's tactics, especially regarding the treatment of innocent women who were brutally raped, beaten, and disfigured by swords. Once Charleston and the surrounding area were firmly secured by the main British army, Tarleton and Ferguson were dispatched on separate missions. Tarleton and his dragoons curbed their abuse of women, but their habit of murdering men who had surrendered actually escalated. These acts of brutality resulted in reciprocal treatment by the Patriots, who on several occasions yelled "Tarleton's quarter," as they too gave no mercy.

As stated previously, when Clinton departed the southern theater and returned to the north, he personally changed Ferguson's assignment from his ad-hoc, composite command to a unique post as the inspector general of the militia. Thus, his temporary rank of lieutenant colonel was ended and Major Ferguson focused on his duties with the Loyalist militia. Again, his endeavors were exemplary; he won favor with his subordinates, and most importantly, his Loyalist militia was soon well-trained, armed, and ready for service.

At the core of Ferguson's newly organized command was a 150-man force from his original "American Volunteers." These soldiers had originally deployed with him at the start of the Southern Campaign, and he relied upon them heavily. His men drew inspiration from their commander, whose morals and professional bearing set a fine example. They were also inspired by his commitment to king and country despite his horrible wounds. Due to Ferguson's qualities as a commander, his men affectionately referred to him as "Bulldog." From this unit, Ferguson assigned Captain Abraham DePeyster (1753–1799) as his second in command. While DePeyster was born and raised in New York, his family was affluent and had deep European roots; thus they remained loyal to Great Britain and their king. Abraham and his brother Frederick both voluntarily served throughout the war as provincial British officers in the Loyalists' American militia. This unit was known collectively as the "Loyal American Volunteers," or the "Provincial Rangers." As Ferguson's second in command, DePeyster was a senior captain by British rank, but his militia or "territorial" rank was that of a colonel. DePeyster

Captain Abraham DePeyster

was a good soldier, devoted to his commander, and he was affectionately known to his men as "the Bulldog's Pup." But in battle, was DePeyster willing to fight as tenaciously as his mentor?

Once drilled and organized along British organizational design, Ferguson's corps of militia went into immediate service. There was no doubt that Patrick Ferguson was a professional and highly capable soldier, yet the abilities of his militia army to wage war remained a great mystery.

While Ferguson trained and drilled his militia in the art of war, several of his subordinate Tory commanders were well known for their opportunistic barbarity. Men such as David Fanning (1755–1825) and the "Bloody Scout" or "Bloody Bill" William Cunningham (?- 1787) were well known in the Carolinas as men of ill repute. Nonetheless, Ferguson employed them, as they had a large following and many people feared them. Besides, Ferguson's mission called for subordinate leaders who knew the region and the partisan enemy, and their ability to rally other Tories to join their cause was invaluable. In his assigned sector, Ferguson worked hard to allay the fears of the locals and to create an air conducive to civility. While several of his militiamen did not help in these matters, Ferguson sincerely tried to be both an officer and a gentleman. Yet, the war being waged was a revolution and while the Loyalist cause in the Carolinas was popular, the Partisan Patriots refused to submit, and the hatred between Tories and Whigs (colonial Patriots) flourished.

With British forces occupying the region, rebellious activity was somewhat quelled, but it never really went away. While the patriotic Whigs faced a rising tide of British domination, these partisan warriors simply awaited opportunities to assail their foe. Several isolated pockets of resistance operated in the remote regions of the South, yet these bands of patriotic forces could achieve little more than occasional raids and ambushes against the king's army. Led by men such as the "Swamp Fox," Francis Marion (1732–1795), and Thomas Sumter (1734–1832), these partisan warriors provided Cornwallis with a constant reminder that opposition still remained. Additionally, while battles were waged by massed troops in the open field, a larger and darker war ensued within the homes of the local citizenry. Bitter hatred between Whigs and Tories further enflamed the politically divided colonists. Both sides passionately embraced their respective causes, and a desperate struggle was waged behind the scenes of the American Revolution. In the remote western regions of the Carolinas and Georgia, resentment was especially acute and violence was the norm. Communities were torn apart as brutal criminal acts were committed by one side against the other. Patriot General Nathaniel Greene (1742–1786) described the situation in North Carolina:

> The animosity between the Whigs and Tories of this State renders their situation truly deplorable. There is not a day passes but there are more or less who fall a sacrifice to this savage disposition. The Whigs seem determined to extirpate the Tories

and the Tories the Whigs. Some thousands have fallen in this way in this quarter, and the evil rages with more violence than ever. If a stop cannot be put to these massacres, the country will be depopulated in a few months more, as neither Whig nor Tory can live.

In the summer of 1780, the Whigs of the Carolinas were outnumbered by the Tories; thus the future looked rather bleak for the Patriot cause. Moreover, Cornwallis boastfully reported to Clinton that all resistance in South Carolina had been terminated. He also reported that in North Carolina there were only 100 Patriot militiamen, commanded by General Charles Caswell, and perhaps 400 to 500 others. However, he also noted that several thousand Patriot troops had entered the state from Virginia, Maryland, and Delaware. Still, Cornwallis felt confident that he could now move northward, and he planned to invade North Carolina in September, intent on "reducing that Province to its duty."

Cornwallis, however, was mistaken in his upbeat appraisal of the situation in the Carolinas. Sumter had assembled a 1,500-man Patriot militia force near Catawba and many other volunteers from Waxhaws and Camden soon joined them. British intelligence also reported to Cornwallis that Patriot General Baron DeKalb (1721–1780) was marching southward with his troops from Maryland and Delaware, followed by another 2,500 militiamen from Virginia. Cornwallis viewed these developments as a natural reaction to his success in the region and felt confident that he could continue his campaign and sweep onward into North Carolina.

As he finalized his plan for moving northward, he strengthened his supply lines throughout South Carolina and built bases in the middle and upper districts. He also strengthened his base at Camden, commanded by Lord Francis Rawdon (1754–1826). British forces at Camden would serve as the base of a fortified hinge while Cornwallis swung his army northward across the border into North Carolina. Ferguson would command his left wing with his army of provincial and Tory militia. Cornwallis in the center would lead the main force of his army into Charlotte Town (Charlotte). Due to continuing clashes with Patriot partisans in the west, Cornwallis also strengthened his fortification at Ninety-Six, which was commanded by Lieutenant Col. John Cruger (1738–1807). With the western flank safely secured, Ferguson's mission was to advance deep into North Carolina, moving into Tryon County (now Rutherford and Lincoln counties), where his Tory militia would rally their neighbors to British allegiance. Ferguson's corps would also secure the mountainous regions in the west and provide protection for the British main advance. As an additional benefit to British forces, Ferguson's presence in the western mountains would also eliminate Patriot incursions southward into District Ninety-Six of South Carolina.

Meanwhile, intelligence reports warned Cornwallis that rebel forces were focusing on Camden. The Patriots had combined the soldiers led by DeKalb with the Carolina forces of General Griffith Rutherford (1721–1805) and General Horatio Gates (1728–1806), who commanded the Patriot army. On August 16 the two armies clashed at the Battle of Camden, resulting in a staggering defeat for the Patriots. Both General DeKalb and General Rutherford were casualties. Gates fled from the field in a hasty retreat and he did not stop until he reached the safety of Hillsboro, North Carolina. American casualties numbered 1,000, while hundreds more were taken prisoner. The Continental Army of the Southern Theater was shattered.

Sumter escaped the field with the largest body of survivors, but Cornwallis sent his dragoons, led by the infamous Lieutenant Col. Banastre "Bloody Ban" Tarleton, to pursue them. On August 18 Tarleton achieved his objective and his men mercilessly destroyed what remained of the

Patriot army. Sumter, known as the "Carolina Gamecock," managed to escape the carnage, but that was the only high-light of a totally disastrous affair. In addition to the human losses suffered by the Patriot army, within two short days they had lost all of their ammunition, seven brass cannons, 130 wagons, and 1,100 rifles; and, as described by the victor, Lord Cornwallis, "in short, there never was a more complete victory." Following the debacle at Camden, General George Washington recorded, "we are tottering on the brink of a precipice." But he also wrote in a letter to a trusted friend, "our case is not desperate, if virtue exists in the people."

Meanwhile, a small battle occurred in the upper northwest corner of South Carolina that was completely overshadowed by the larger events of the day. In the dark early morning hours of August 18, a battle between Patriot partisans and British forces erupted at Musgrove's Mill on the Enoree River. While the event has received little mention in history, it involved key combatants who played important roles later in the war. Georgian Elijah Clarke, South Carolinian James Williams, and the future "Overmountain" leaders Isaac Shelby and John Sevier led the Partisan warriors in the frontier region of the Carolinas. These virtuous men employed the tactics of frontier rangers and they fought like wild Indians. This band of Patriots had been wreaking havoc in the "up-country" of South Carolina and making the British look bad. Stealthily, they had moved into a position to strike at elements of Ferguson's Corps located at Musgrove's Mill. In a sudden attack that caught Ferguson's men off guard, the Patriots quickly inflicted nearly 200 casualties, then withdrew with only a dozen casualties of their own. Capt. Abraham DePeyster noted that the backwoods Patriots were tenacious fighters and, because of their Indian-like tactics and intimidating war whoops, he referred to them as those "damned yelling boys." The victorious Patriots seemingly "disappeared" into the forest whence they came. Expecting the larger British force to pursue them, the Patriots withdrew from the scene of battle. Clarke and his Georgians moved southwest toward their homes, while the remaining partisan warriors fled northward into the refuge of the North Carolina hills.

These partisan frontiersmen were experienced warriors and their leaders were exceptionally gifted at waging a revolutionary war. Elijah Clarke (1733–1807) was from Wilkes County, Georgia, and was probably the most determined guerrilla fighter in the Southern Theater. He was unrelenting in his attacks on the British and Indians, especially around Augusta and District Ninety-Six in South Carolina. He survived multiple wounds and captivity, and he selflessly sacrificed his own personal safety for the people he loved. His band of Georgians paid dearly for their achievements, and in their failures their costs were in the extreme. Numerous members of his community, including women and children, were savagely tortured and killed by Indians allied with the British. It is likely that more of Clarke's soldiers were summarily hanged than those of any other partisan command. Yet, despite numerous setbacks, Clarke always returned to fight his foe. For his diligent efforts, he was one of the most eagerly sought rebels in the South. Because of Ferguson's obsession to capture him, Clarke unwittingly played a key role in Ferguson's ultimate fate.

One of Clarke's neighbors from across the border in South Carolina was also a determined Patriot. Col. James Williams (1740–1780) was a proud South Carolinian and a veteran soldier. He had served as an officer in Sumter's command during earlier campaigns of the war, and he had amassed a well-known reputation as "rough, rash and fearless." Yet he frequently clashed with his compatriots as well. Despite his shortcomings, Williams was a devout Patriot and when called upon at King's Mountain, he "poured out his blood" for his country.

While Clarke and Williams were good warriors, Cols. John Sevier and Isaac Shelby were two of the most naturally gifted and admired leaders on the frontier. The two men had a great deal in common. John Sevier (1745–1851) and

Colonel John Sevier   **Colonel Isaac Shelby**

Isaac Shelby (1745–1826) were both born and raised in the wilderness. They grew up living off the land, hunting, planting, building settlements, fighting Indians, and they were both respected members of the local militia. In 1771, they both settled in a region of what is now northeast Tennessee that was then a remote frontier section of North Carolina. While they lived in different settlements and counties, their homes were just eighteen miles apart. Shelby lived in Sullivan County, in a place called Sapling Grove (now known as Bristol). His father, Evan Shelby Sr., was the local militia commander. Thus Isaac was raised as a soldier, lived in a fort, and served under his father's command. Sevier lived on the banks of the Holston River (near present day Kingsport), where Indians were a constant threat and hardships were a way of life. While Sevier was five years older than his friend Shelby was, their lives ran parallel courses. As they matured into manhood, their martial skills and leadership abilities naturally led them into military service. They both received commissions as officers in 1774; and since their combat experiences involved frontier battles with the Indians, their abilities as partisan warriors were well refined. The men who served under Shelby and Sevier had seen them fight, they respected them, and they proudly followed them into battle. Simply put, both of these men exemplified the term "freedom fighter," but how would they fare in battle against the army of Great Britain?

With the Patriots' retreat from District Ninety-Six, and the British victory at Camden, Cornwallis was secure in his belief that South Carolina was a conquered region. In accordance with his lordship's plan, North Carolina was next, and Cornwallis was eager to move. The British victors were greatly encouraged by their destruction of the Patriot army at Camden, which also bolstered the morale of the Loyalist militia. As a professional soldier, Cornwallis never cared much for the militia, but upon learning that some of the Patriot combatants in the Battle of Camden had previously served the Crown, he reacted too harshly. He ordered his men to immediately hang any traitors, to imprison those individuals who displayed opposition to British authority, and to impound or destroy their belongings. Cornwallis also sent word throughout the Carolinas that the same measures applied to everyone. These desperate and hastily conceived orders would later haunt Cornwallis, but for the time being, he followed up his victory with a renewed vigor to conquer North Carolina. He also sent word into North Carolina urging Loyalist allies to assist the British forces by capturing suspected rebels, seizing their arms and ammunition, and preparing for the arrival of his army.

Meanwhile, Maj. Patrick Ferguson's corps of Loyalist militia and provincial Redcoats deployed into the rugged western foothills of North Carolina. The movements of his army were short and cautious and Ferguson made no attempt to pursue the partisans who had attacked his forces at Musgrove's Mill. Nonetheless, both the Patriot and Tory forces proceeded to the same location—Gilbert Town, North Carolina (near present-day Rutherfordton). While Ferguson's force was actually several days' march behind the partisan forces, the Patriots believed that Ferguson was hot on their trail. Thus, the Patriots hastily met in Gilbert Town to discuss their future activities, while Colonel Williams continued on to Hillsboro with British prisoners captured at Musgrove's Mill. Isaac Shelby and John Sevier proposed that they should all return to their homes and gather larger forces. They also suggested that perhaps the men from southwest North Carolina should join them on the other side of the Blue Ridge Mountains. Then, once their families were safe there, they could re-form their army and return to fight the British with adequate strength. Andrew Hampton and the McDowell brothers from nearby Quaker Meadows in Burke County, experienced guerrilla fighters who led the local Patriots, embraced the plan of Shelby and Sevier. Additionally, the Patriots decided to communicate their plan to Col. Benjamin Cleveland, commander of friendly forces in Surry and Wilkes County. With a plan for future action secured, Shelby, Sevier, and their men returned to their homes across the mountains. Meanwhile, Charles and Joseph McDowell prepared for the inevitable arrival of Ferguson and his Tory accomplices.

On September 7, Ferguson led a detachment of fifty provincial Redcoats and 300 Tory militiamen into Gilbert Town. Ferguson faced no resistance from Patriot forces. The McDowell clan followed the advice of their "backwater" (the area across the mountains where the rivers drained west instead of east) friends, and they too "disappeared" into the safety of the mountains. For many locals, the mere sight of Redcoats and Tories massed on North Carolina soil persuaded them to favor allegiance to the king, and many of them joined Ferguson's army. Encouraged by his success in the region, Ferguson decided to address the people across the mountains as well. Ferguson selected Samuel Phillips, a

Major Patrick Ferguson's headquarters outside Gilbert Town, North Carolina

rebel captive from the "backwater" region, to deliver a message to the frontier Patriots on the other side of the Blue Ridge Mountains. Incidentally, Phillips happened to be the cousin of Patriot leader Isaac Shelby. Ferguson's message was a threatening ultimatum, and it played a pivotal role in future events. Ferguson told them that if they did not desist from their opposition to the British arms, and "take protection under his standard, he would march his army over the mountains, hang their leaders, and lay their country waste with fire and sword."

Phillips raced across the mountains carrying Ferguson's infamous message, while the British chieftain scoured the region for rebel hideouts. Ferguson marched his army northward into Burke County, where his men skirmished with the trailing element of McDowell's force, who narrowly escaped into the high country. Ferguson's corps then swept across the Catawba and Broad Rivers and returned to Gilbert Town on September 23. Within two weeks Ferguson

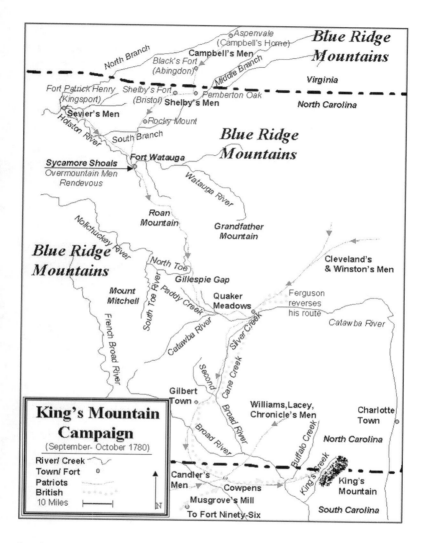

had enlisted at least 500 Tory militiamen and swept the region of rebel forces, and he briefly relaxed in the security of his success. Ferguson then received intelligence from Fort Ninety-Six that rebel leader Elijah Clarke was retreating into his vicinity. Accordingly, Ferguson deployed his army to the southwest along the Green River in hopes of catching

Clarke and his rebels in that sector. Ultimately, Ferguson never saw Clarke or any of his Georgia partisans, yet he spent a lot of time "chasing ghosts," and the wasted time would soon haunt him. Ferguson had received alarming news that the Overmountain men were approaching and he suddenly called off the hunt for Clarke and rode hard to the east. On October 1, when he felt safe in Tryon County at Denard's Ford on the banks of the Broad River, Ferguson issued another inflammatory proclamation. His message, which he had posted throughout the countryside, challenged the local inhabitants to rally in support of the Crown. He also warned them with:

> Gentlemen: Unless you wish to be eat up by an inundation of barbarians, who have begun by murdering an unarmed son before the aged father, and afterwards lopped off his arms, and who by their shocking cruelties and irregularities, give the best proof of their cowardice and want of discipline; I say, if you wish to be pinioned, robbed, and murdered, and see your wives and daughters, in four days, abused by the dregs of mankind—in short, if you wish or deserve to bear the name of men, grasp your arms in a moment and run to camp.
>
> The backwater men have crossed the mountains; McDowell, Hampton, Shelby, and Cleveland are at their head, so that you know what you have to depend upon. If you choose to be pissed upon forever and ever by a set of mongrels, say so at once, and let your women turn their backs upon you, and look out for real men to protect them.
>
> –Pat Ferguson, Major, Seventy-first Regiment.

Ferguson's words conveyed a challenging tone and they stirred emotions on both sides of the conflict. His challenge simply fanned the flames of American patriotism and strengthened the rebels' resolve throughout the western

Carolinas. As Ferguson mentioned in his "pissing" proclamation, he had received news of the impending movements of the "backwater" men. Tory spies and Patriot deserters reported to Ferguson that the "Overmountain Men" were hell-bent on destroying him and his army. Perhaps the bravado in Ferguson's speech masked his personal anxiety concerning his approaching enemies, as he also sent an urgent message to Fort Ninety-Six. This message urged Colonel Cruger to immediately call out two regiments of militia and to send them forward as reinforcements.

After Ferguson's first message, relayed by paroled prisoner Sam Phillips, was delivered, the Patriot leaders got busy preparing a response. Phillips delivered Ferguson's message to Isaac Shelby at his fort on Sapling Grove (now Bristol, Tennessee). Shelby then conferred with his fellow Patriot commanders in the region, John Sevier, the McDowell brothers who were living in the Watauga Valley as refugees, and Col. William Campbell, who would be difficult to persuade. Still, Shelby knew that Campbell's participation was crucial to the task at hand and he worked diligently to win his assistance.

Like his neighbors John Sevier and Isaac Shelby, William Campbell (1745–1781) was born and bred in a lifestyle that forged men into rough and self-reliant soldiers. He too was an experienced backwoodsman and Indian fighter, but he was better educated, more experienced, and burdened with more responsibilities than Sevier and Shelby. Although Campbell was the same age as Sevier, he had settled in Washington County, Virginia, near Abingdon, and thus lived about twenty miles northeast of his compatriot neighbors. Campbell knew John Sevier and he had campaigned with Isaac Shelby as militia captains under the command of Isaac's father, Col. Evan Shelby Sr. Campbell also served as a Washington County judge and he held appointments to other civic duties as well. Thus, between his military campaigns and his judicial and other civic duties, Campbell was a busy man and a leading pillar of

**Colonel William Campbell;
portrait by Robert Wilson**

his community. Campbell's roots originated in Scotland, but his commitment to wresting freedom from Great Britain was vehement and displayed much earlier than in most Patriots. Lord Dunmore, the British colonial governor of Virginia, frequently wronged Campbell and his fellow frontiersmen. In January 1775, Campbell and his compatriots sent a message to the newly formed Continental Congress stating that as free men, their rights would not be trampled upon. In an excerpt from their declaration, these early patriots recorded that:

> We declare that we are deliberately and resolutely determined never to surrender them to any power upon earth but at the expense of our lives. These are our real, though unpolished, sentiments of liberty and loyalty, and in them we are resolved to live and die.

After the battles of Lexington and Concord in Massachusetts, Campbell was among the first to volunteer for the Continental Army. In September 1775, he traveled to Williamsburg, where he was commissioned a captain in the First Virginia Regiment, under the command of the fiery but eloquent Patriot, the Rev. Patrick Henry. Campbell and his commander forged a lasting friendship and obviously they shared many beliefs. When stationed at Williamsburg, Campbell was thirty years old and a very eligible bachelor. He is described as a very large, but handsome man. He had red hair and blue eyes and he was very personable. During the course of the next year, he fell in love with Henry's sister and they were married.

Shortly thereafter, the events that "turned the world upside down" exploded throughout the newly formed nation. Patrick Henry became the first governor of the newly formed Commonwealth of Virginia, Campbell fought battles against the British near Hampton, and back home on the frontier the Indians were attacking settlers in the western backwoods region. Campbell reluctantly left the Continental Line and returned to the frontier with his young bride. The young couple established a home in Aspenvale, forty miles northeast of the present Bristol, Virginia. Back at home, Campbell quickly ascended in rank to colonel and continued his work as a part-time judge, and he and his wife started a family. The Indians were encouraged by the British to attack the Patriots in the frontier, while Tories threatened the lead mines in southwest Virginia (critical to the Patriot cause). After Thomas Jefferson succeeded Patrick Henry as governor, he too saw the talents of Campbell and soon had him chasing Tories, Indians, and the British. Thus, when Shelby elicited the assistance of Campbell for his mission into North Carolina to pursue Ferguson, Campbell showed some initial reluctance. Still, he saw the merit in the venture and agreed to help. Ultimately, not only did Campbell help, he contributed more men to the endeavor, bore the brunt of the fighting at King's Mountain, and paid more dearly in blood than any other Patriot commander.

Once the details were finalized, the "Overmountain Men" initiated their plan to march over the mountains and eliminate the threat posed by Ferguson and his Loyalist militia. The route, known today as the "Overmountain Trail," began at a pasture called Dunn's Meadows in Abingdon, Virginia. Here Colonel Campbell assembled his men and they traveled towards Shelby's Fort to join with Isaac Shelby and his men.

The following day the mounted militiamen crossed the Holston River, passing the frontier post of Rocky Mount, and they culminated the first leg of their journey at Sycamore Shoals (just below the present town of Elizabethton, Tennessee) on the banks of the Watauga River. Here the forces of Sevier, McDowell, Campbell, and Shelby gathered their composite forces on September 25, 1780.

The gathering of the "Overmountain Men" was a massive rally of frontier pioneers who assembled to create a partisan Patriot army. The volunteers arrived in droves and their women assisted them by preparing food and supplies. One intrepid lady, Mary McKeehan Patton, supplied the partisan army with 500 pounds of gunpowder that she personally prepared. This was a risky endeavor, due not only to the inherent dangers of mixing gunpowder, but in the eyes of the British authorities, it was illegal. Sweating over a large cast iron kettle, her difficult and meticulous labors filled the Patriots' powder horns with high-quality, fast-burning gunpowder. These patriotic men were a hardy breed, tough as leather, long-haired backwoodsmen with lean bodies and stern dispositions. While they were backwoods settlers, their ranks were filled with pioneer founders of our nation, future governors, senators, and congressmen. Several of them were fathers of future American icons, such as John Crockett, whose son Davy would become a frontier hero. There were at least four black men among the patriots, and while these men traditionally performed subservient labors, they were capable fighters as well. In fact, so many men volunteered for serv-

"Gathering of the Overmountain Men at Sycamore Shoals" by Lloyd Branson; courtesy of the Tennessee State Museum

ice, they had to reduce their numbers. The settlements could ill afford to send too many men, as the threat from Indians was omnipresent on the frontier. From the assembled forces the following commanders and their respective numbers were chosen to embark on the following day:

- Col. William Campbell—400 Virginia militia (Washington County, Virginia)
- Col. Isaac Shelby—240 men from Sullivan County, North Carolina (now Tennessee)
- Col. John Sevier—240 men from Washington County, North Carolina (now Tennessee)
- Maj. Joseph McDowell—120 men from Burke County, North Carolina

Before departing, the assembled force received a sermon delivered by the Rev. Samuel Doak. He asked that God accompany the men on their expedition, to bless them with strength and courage, and when facing their foe to wield the "sword of the Lord and Gideon." The partisan warriors echoed the phrase, said their good-byes, mounted their horses, and began the pursuit of their foe.

Col. Charles McDowell (1743–1815) rode ahead of the main body to inform Col. Benjamin Cleveland (1738–1806) and other friendly forces that the Patriot army was en route across the mountains. With heights ranging from five to six thousand feet, the journey across the mountains was an arduous one, but these men were rugged and accustomed to life in the mountain wilderness. As they crossed the frigid heights of Roan Mountain, it was encrusted with an early snow, but as they descended through the lower river valleys, the weather was clear and mild. The journey was undoubtedly beautiful as fall was in its full splendor. The men camped by night and rode hard, long days, covering between fifteen and twenty-five miles per day.

On the evening of September 30, the Overmountain Men arrived at Quaker Meadows in North Carolina and the home of the McDowell family. Here Col. Benjamin Cleveland and Maj. Joseph Winston's force of 350 men from Wilkes and Surry counties joined the Patriot army.

Benjamin Cleveland was the eldest of the commanders in the composite Patriot force chasing Ferguson and his Loyalist militia. With forty-two years of hard living behind him, Cleveland was an ardent Patriot and a very active leader in the Patriot cause. Like his peers, Charles McDowell and James Williams, he remained active in the field. And like all of the Patriots assembled, Cleveland was born and raised on the frontier, and he had well-honed skills as a hunter, Indian fighter, and Patriot partisan. While he was originally from Virginia, he migrated to North Carolina in 1769. In addition to being an avid military officer, he was also very active in civic duties as a judge and bondsman, and he served in the State Senate as a representative of Wilkes County. He fought diligently to keep Tories clear of the area around Surry and Wilkes Counties, and he quickly ascended to the rank of colonel.

Cleveland's men were very loyal to their leader, who was a very large man and whom they affectionately called "Old Round-About." Likewise, Cleveland was devoutly attached

Major Joseph Winston

to his men, who were known locally as "Cleveland's Devils." Their title may have reflected their leader's war philosophy concerning Tories, which was to "give them hell" and hang them to "get them out of their misery." While Cleveland had a reputation as a brutal man, warfare in this region was waged savagely. Cleveland's compatriot leading the forces from Surry County was Maj. Joseph Winston (1746–1815). Winston also grew up fighting Indians in the frontier, and he joined the military in 1775. He was a very active militia officer and fought in numerous campaigns throughout the war, including frequent service with his neighboring commander, Colonel Cleveland. Combined once more for another campaign against the Tories, the 350 men of Surry and Wilkes added greatly to the Patriots' task at hand.

The next day, October 1, the Patriot army pressed forward with greater strength and they made better headway as the terrain leveled out below the mountains. That evening, however, powerful rains signaled the beginning of an ominous storm. The Patriots were within sixteen miles of Gilbert Town, and they were uncertain as to where

Ferguson was located. The storm was so great that the men remained in camp through the next day. That evening the commanders of the various Patriot forces held an important conference.

The senior officers were all colonels, and they knew someone should take charge as the senior commander. Shelby and Sevier just wanted to get on with the task at hand, but they did not want the elders, Cols. Charles McDowell or Benjamin Cleveland, in charge. Both of these men were considered to be "too old and slow." Shelby convinced Col. William Campbell to take the job, as he was the only one there from a different colony, he was the most experienced soldier, and he had the largest command. McDowell bowed out gracefully, and he departed for Hillsboro in search of assistance from the Continental Army. His command devolved to his younger brother, Maj. Joseph McDowell (1758–1799), while Cleveland, with a smaller command, yielded to the commanders of the larger force. The officers also decided that, while Campbell was in charge of the campaign, they would jointly discuss major decisions. With their command dilemma resolved, they proceeded on their quest for Ferguson and arrived in Gilbert Town on October 4. Here, they fully expected to encounter their foe, but upon their arrival they learned that Ferguson was not there. Ferguson had spread word, via a ruse, that he was heading his force southwest towards Fort Ninety-Six. Actually, he was heading southeast towards Charlotte Town and the safety of Lord Cornwallis and the main British army.

The Patriots immediately moved southward and reached Cowpens, South Carolina, on the evening of October 6, where they were joined by additional friendly forces. Col. James Williams arrived with 400 additional men from the Carolinas. These men also consisted of a composite force, as they were remnants of Sumter's South Carolina partisans, led by Cols. William Hill and Edward Lacey, and members of Col. William Graham's North Carolinians, commanded by Lt. Col. Frederick Hambright and Maj.

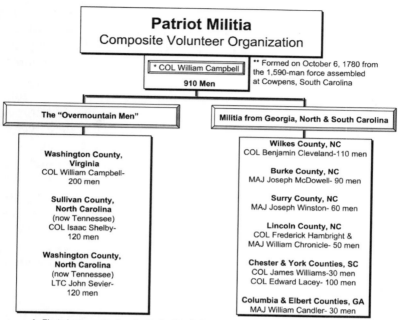

Patriot Militia
Composite Volunteer Organization

* COL William Campbell
910 Men

** Formed on October 6, 1780 from the 1,590-man force assembled at Cowpens, South Carolina

The "Overmountain Men"	Militia from Georgia, North & South Carolina
Washington County, Virginia COL William Campbell- 200 men **Sullivan County, North Carolina** (now Tennessee) COL Isaac Shelby- 120 men **Washington County, North Carolina** (now Tennessee) LTC John Sevier- 120 men	**Wilkes County, NC** COL Benjamin Cleveland-110 men **Burke County, NC** MAJ Joseph McDowell- 90 men **Surry County, NC** MAJ Joseph Winston- 60 men **Lincoln County, NC** COL Frederick Hambright & MAJ William Chronicle- 50 men **Chester & York Counties, SC** COL James Williams-30 men COL Edward Lacey- 100 men **Columbia & Elbert Counties, GA** MAJ William Candler- 30 men

* Elected commander from the leadership of all units assembled.
** These units comprised the "mounted" troops selected for the attack on Ferguson's Tory Militia.

William Chronicle. An isolated thirty-man element of Clarke's men, commanded by Maj. William Candler, had heard about the approaching Patriots, and they too joined the Patriot forces.

Colonel Williams brought yet another crisis of command to the situation, as he was holding a newly appointed commission as a militia general. However, there was no time for argument at this point. The commanders held an immediate council, where it was decided that Campbell would retain command of the composite forces, and they formulated an immediate plan of action. The newly arrived forces informed their fellow Patriots that Ferguson was located near Cherokee Ford on the Broad River. Apparently, Ferguson's corps was moving east towards the safety of Charlotte Town. They also learned that "Bloody Bill" Cunningham, Col. Zachariah Gibbs, and six hundred Tory militiamen were camped just six miles south of Cowpens. The Patriot leaders chose to ignore the report concerning Cunningham and focused their attention on their original goal. An immediate pursuit was planned and the colonels decided to organize a swift-moving force of the best horsemen to move out at once. The remaining troops would follow the next day and move as rapidly as they could behind the main force, although many of the horses were weak and some men had no mounts. The Patriots were already exhausted from a hard day's ride, but with the ominous situation, their excitement pushed them onward. At 8 P.M., the 910-man force designated to lead the pursuit moved out in a driving rain. Time was critical, as each moment of delay put them closer toward the possibility that Ferguson would escape them, or even worse, that Cornwallis could reach Ferguson with reinforcements. Uncertainty loomed heavily in their hearts.

Unbeknownst to the Patriot army, Ferguson was trying to determine exactly what he should do. He dispatched numerous messengers seeking information from his allies. A large detachment of his Tory militia, led by Colonel Gibbs and "Bloody Bill" Cunningham, was sweeping through the countryside gathering troops and supplies, but he had no contact with them. While the Patriots knew their whereabouts, that particular band of Tories remained unaware of the drama swirling around them. In consequence, they did not assist Ferguson, nor did they have a role in the impending conflict. While Ferguson knew the "Overmountain Men" were hot on his trail, he was uncertain as to their exact strength and mistakenly surmised that Clarke's rebel forces had joined his pursuers. In a message to Cornwallis, on October 5, Ferguson stated, "I am on my march towards you, by a road leading from Cherokee Ford, north of King's Mountain. Three or four hundred good soldiers, part dragoons, would finish the business. Something must be done soon. This is their last push in this quarter." Along his retreat toward Charlotte Town, Ferguson apparently decided that the Patriot threat was not as ominous as suspected. If he had continued his retreat to Charlotte, Ferguson could have escaped his pursuers, but again he simply did not know for certain where they were, nor how close.

Meanwhile, Ferguson received word from Colonel Cruger at Fort Ninety-Six that no reinforcements were available. Ferguson then made a decision to make a stand against his foe. We may never know for certain why he made it: He may have expected Cunningham's force to return, or perhaps he thought that Cornwallis would send Tarleton to his aid. Maybe, he simply decided to fight the men he considered to be contemptible "backwater banditti." Nonetheless, Ferguson marched his army southward, making a deliberate hook maneuver onto a ridgeline thirty-six miles west of Charlotte. Ferguson chose to establish his forces in a defensive posture on what his adjutant, Anthony Allaire (1755–1838), referred to as "Little King's Mountain." (Just to the northeast there is a larger mountain in the chain that is sometimes mistakenly referred to as King's Mountain, but it is known locally as "the Pinnacle." King's Mountain is the same mountain Allaire referred to as "Little King's Mountain.")

Ferguson chose King's Mountain for his defense apparently because it had enough room to accommodate his entire forces. Upon the crest of King's Mountain, a small plateau 600 yards long extends from the northeast, where it is 120 feet wide to the southwest, where it narrows to a width of 70 feet. In the northeast corner of the mountain, Ferguson parked his seventeen wagons in a semicircle facing north, and he established his headquarters and encampment in this area. Once established on the heights, Ferguson must have felt secure in his position, or at least he stated that for the benefit of his men, as he reportedly declared, "He was on King's Mountain, that he was king of that mountain, and God Almighty could not drive him from it." Another rendition of Ferguson's arrogant boast

Lieutenant Anthony Allaire

states that he declared, "All the rebels in hell could not push him off." Despite whatever Ferguson may have said to his men, his written correspondence reflects a degree of uncertainty. With his force established on the heights, on October 6, Ferguson wrote his final message to Cornwallis, stating, "My Lordship, I arrived today at King's Mountain and have taken a post where I do not think I can be faced by a stronger enemy than that against us." The body of the message has never been fully decrypted, but within the legible text there are clear references that acknowledge Ferguson's realization that reinforcements would not be arriving from Colonel Cruger at Fort Ninety-Six. Moreover, Ferguson stated (very weakly) that Tarleton and "a few real dragoons" would "enable us to act decisively and vigorously." This last statement, coupled with additional messages to Tarleton, indicate that Ferguson would certainly welcome any assistance available.

While Ferguson expressed the opinion that Tarleton's dragoons would help the situation, he did not venture a definitive request for assistance. Additionally, if Ferguson had known that Tarleton was ill, bed-ridden, and totally ignorant of Ferguson's predicament, his tone may have expressed more apprehension. Ultimately, Ferguson and the fate of his corps were quite hazardously perched in a precarious uncertainty, and there was little "his Lordship" or anyone else could do for them.

Meanwhile, at dawn on October 7, the 910-man Patriot force arrived at Cherokee Ford on the banks of the Broad River. The partisan leaders employed scouts throughout their journey and once the far side of the river was declared free of enemy forces, they crossed the swollen river. The night march had been difficult and circuitous, and the heavy rain was still pouring. After crossing the river, several of the Patriot leaders halted and discussed the merits of a much-needed rest. Shelby lost his temper and yelled furiously, "I will not stop until night, if I follow Ferguson into Cornwallis' lines!" Without a reply, the colonels spurred their mounts and continued their mission. After several more miles, the Patriots were forced to halt as several horses reached exhaustion, and the men were also eager to rest. Near Cashion's Crossroads, the main force halted for a brief respite while their scouts reconnoitered the road ahead. By noon the rain ended, the sun appeared, and the Patriots received even brighter news in the form of intelligence concerning their enemy. The local inhabitants were well aware that Ferguson's army was located just ahead of the Patriots on King's Mountain. A local woman had even delivered chickens to their camp the day before, and several Tory sympathizers confirmed the information.

Continuing their travel along a northeast trail that ran parallel to the ridgeline, the Patriots soon passed Antioch Church, and another halt was ordered within five miles of the reported enemy position. More information was received from the locals concerning Ferguson's position, including additional details about the camp layout and disposition of the enemy forces. As the Patriots neared Ponder's Creek and the Ponder family's homestead,

Colonel Hambright noticed a young 14-year-old boy named John Ponder riding by on his horse and looking suspicious. Hambright had his men arrest the youth, as he knew his brother was a Tory soldier. Ponder was serving Ferguson as a messenger and the Patriots confiscated his dispatches, including one addressed to Lord Cornwallis. While the message included some elements written in a secret code, the Patriots were able to discern enough to verify Ferguson's situation. The messenger also provided them with a good description of his commander and the enemy's disposition. According to the youth, his commander was the best-uniformed man on the mountain, but "they could not see his military suit, as he wore a checked shirt, or duster, over it."

This valuable information was disseminated to the Patriot troops, and Colonel Hambright encouraged the men to "mark him with your rifles." After crossing Ponder's Creek, the mud-covered colonial trail (present day South Carolina Highway 216) turned southward towards the ridgeline and Yorkville, South Carolina, which lies beyond the heights. After crossing the lower branch of King's Creek, the road begins an ascent into the mountains. To the Mountain Men, these heights were more akin to hills, as the highest elevations in this part of the ridge average a mere 1,000 feet. After a gradual incline for about 2,500 feet, the road passes between two knobs, where the terrain levels off into a short plateau. From this position, just 800 meters away, the Patriot partisans could view the broad side or northern slopes of King's Mountain. Veiled by the thick forest they could not see their enemy, and thus far the Patriots had retained the important element of surprise. Stealthily, the Patriots moved down into a ravine below the road, completed their plan, and prepared for battle.

2

THE BATTLE OF KING'S MOUNTAIN

SAFELY CONCEALED WITHIN A THICKLY wooded ravine, Col. William Campbell and his partisan commanders completed a tactical plan of assault, while their men prepared themselves for battle. Several of Major Chronicle's men had hunted in this area and they imparted descriptions of the terrain held by the enemy. With this information, the commanders decided to encircle the enemy positions, assault from all directions, and force the enemy into an ever-shrinking kill zone. In a move to improve command and control throughout the mission, they divided their force into two divisions of nearly equal strength.

These two divisions were further divided into four linear columns so they could maintain unit integrity throughout movement to the objective and rapidly achieve their respective assault positions. The "Left Division," with two columns, would surround the base of the mountain on the north side of the objective, while the "Right Division" would do the same in the south. The northern "Left Division" was organized from left (southwest) to right (northeast) as follows: Colonel Shelby's 120 men; the composite force of Colonel William's thirty men, Colonel Lacey's 100 men, and Major Candler's thirty men; then Colonel Cleveland's 110 men, and the fifty men commanded by Colonel Hambright and Major Chronicle. The southern "Right Division" was organized from left (southwest) to right (northeast) as follows: Colonel Campbell's 200 men, Colonel Sevier's 120 men, then Major McDowell's ninety men and Major Winston's sixty men. Thus, the left division on the northern face of the mountain would assault the heights with 440 men, while 470 men would attack the southern slopes. Once Shelby and Campbell's forces were in position, they were to signal the commencement of the assault by yelling their infamous Indian war-whoops. Once the battle had begun, everyone was to press upwards simultaneously. All of the commanders agreed with the plan. Thus, on October 7, 1780, at approximately 2 P.M., the leaders returned to their respective commands, informed their men of the plan, and prepared to move out.

As the columns prepared to march, Colonel Campbell visited each unit, informing them "that if any of them, men or officers, were afraid, to quit the ranks and go home; that he wished no man to engage in the action who could not fight; that as for himself, he was determined to fight the enemy a week, if need be, to gain the victory." The separate commanders gave spirited speeches to encourage their men. Colonel Cleveland's remarks capture the sentiment of them all as he stated:

> My brave fellows, we have beat the Tories, and we can beat them again. They are all cowards; if they had the spirit of men they would join their fellow citizens in supporting the independence of their country. When you are engaged, you are not to wait for the word of command from me. I will show you by example how to fight; I can undertake no more. Every man must consider himself an officer, and act from his own judgment. Fire as quick as you can. When you can do no better, get behind trees, or retreat; but I beg you not to run quite off. If we are repulsed let us make a point of returning and renewing the fight; perhaps we may have better luck in the second attempt than in the first. If any of

you are afraid, such shall leave to retire, and they are requested immediately to take themselves off.

Throughout the columns, some men placed pieces of paper or cloth in their hats to designate themselves as Patriots (Tories used boughs of evergreen). Some of the partisan warriors viewed any form of headgear as an encumbrance; thus they removed their hats and fought Indian style. Then the final orders were given, "Tie up overcoats, pick touch-holes, fresh prime, and be ready to fight." Most of the Patriots were armed with Deckard rifles, commonly referred to as the Pennsylvania or Kentucky Long Rifle. These men were experts with their rifles and they could shoot accurately at distances approaching 300 yards. The commands of their officers were to check their weapons one final time, and "fresh prime" insured that their rifles were ready to fire. A final check of their essential tools, knife, tomahawk, shot bags, and powder horns was followed by the placement of four or five lead balls in their cheeks for quick access and reloading on the move. While the men had ridden hard and not slept for thirty-six hours, an autonomous surge of adrenaline and a quickening of their pulse rejuvenated their exhausted bodies. James Collins, a young partisan serving under Major Chronicle, recorded, "My feelings were not the most pleasant. They may be attributed to my youth, not being quite seventeen . . . but I could not well swallow the appellation of coward."

The rain had ended and the trees in their autumn splendor rustled in the cool gentle breezes. Above them, the sun peeked through the forest, occasionally providing glimpses of movement on the towering heights above. Colonel Campbell gave the order to commence movement and Maj. Joseph Winston led his men out first. His job was to ride hard, swing way around to the southwest of the ridge, making an arc about a mile beyond the mountain, circle back, and approach the objective from the northeast. Winston's mission was perceived as critical because the

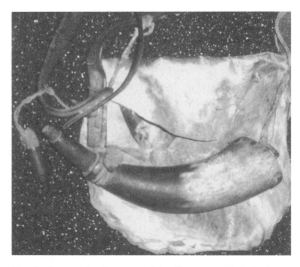

Typical powder horn and leather pouch (shot bag) carried by frontier soldiers

eastern side of the mountain contained the only road to the heights. Thus, if Ferguson attempted a retreat from the mountain and an escape towards Charlotte, Winston's force would block his move. At least this was the plan, and off the men rode.

The Patriot commanders sent scouts on foot ahead of their mounted columns to eliminate any sentries that Ferguson may have posted. In his column, Shelby directed the scouts to search an area he suspected to be manned. His scouts were armed with the close-killing tools of the Indian. The "Overmountain Men" were all skilled in the use of the tomahawk and scalping knife, as they had honed their craft from years of fighting the experts. The rain-soaked floor of the forest combined with the breezy wind rustling the leaves overhead, and Shelby's warriors enjoyed perfect conditions for masking their movement. In short order, Shelby's intuition was verified. His scouts stealthily approached Ferguson's sentries and felled them silently. About the same time, one of Campbell's scouts,

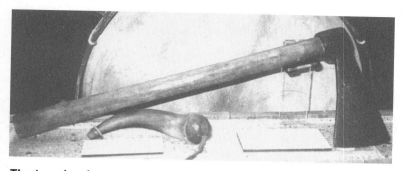

**The tomahawk was adopted by frontiersmen from the Cherokee
Indians and it was a popular weapon among the Overmountain Men.**

Joseph Starnes, also killed a sentry "without giving the
least alarm," and these achievements were viewed as a
"good omen." Thus far, the partisan Patriots retained the
key element of surprise, and seemingly everything was
going perfectly.

Meanwhile, in the tranquil mountain encampment
above, rows of white British tents gently waved in the
afternoon breeze. In camp Ferguson's laundry and cooking
was being tended to by his two women , Virginia Sal and
Virginia Paul. These two young ladies were reported to be
very attractive and they were apparently Ferguson's "mis-
tresses" as well. In addition to his lady friends, Ferguson's
headquarters also contained three surgeons, two adjutants,
one orderly, and one drummer. His official roster of
October 7, 1780, indicates that his army numbered 1,125.
These men were busily engaged in preparing for battle and
guarding Ferguson's mountain stronghold. His Tory adjutant, Alexander Chesney, an Irishman with previous service as a Patriot officer, was making an inspection of the
militia positions, both above and below the heights.
Ferguson was most likely preoccupied with his situation,
as he had no intelligence concerning the whereabouts of
the "backwater men" and their fellow "banditti." He also
had not received any messages from Lord Cornwallis or
Colonel Tarleton, and apparently he had lost contact with

Major Patrick Ferguson

his Loyalists comrades led by Col. Zachariah Gibbs and "Bloody Bill" Cunningham.

Ferguson could certainly have used the additional strength of Gibbs's force, but there was little room for them on King's Mountain. The British tents and wagons occupied the northeastern corner of the mountain, while Ferguson had placed his army stretched out along the ridge's long, narrow, and barren plateau. Additionally, at strategic locations below the heights, Ferguson had dispatched sentries to provide for early warning. Due to illnesses and various external assignments to outposts like Fort Ninety-Six, Ferguson's red-coated "Provincial Rangers," commanded by Capt. Abraham DePeyster, had dwindled to seventy-five men. Capt. Samuel Ryerson assisted DePeyster in the supervision of these trusted soldiers, known collectively as the "Loyal American Volunteers." Ferguson relied on these experienced troops as the backbone of his army.

In the ranks of the Loyalist militia, Ferguson's Corps was comprised of elements of six regiments, organized into four main units. The bulk of his militia had been raised in

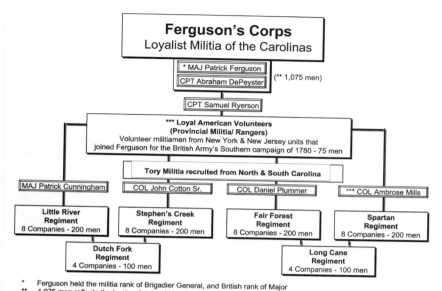

and around District Ninety-Six in South Carolina, but as Ferguson moved through North Carolina, he gathered many additional forces. Thus, there are no known records of the exact composition of these Loyalist militia units, but historical records indicate that on October 7, 1780, at least four Tory colonels and a senior major were posted on King's Mountain. Analysis of the various fragmentary reports and militia-related records indicate that the commanders and their respective units were organized as follows: Col. Ambrose Mills, commander of the Spartan Regiment and several companies of the Long Cane Regiment; Col. Daniel Plummer, commander of the Fair Forest Regiment and several companies of the Long Cane Regiment; Col. John Cotton Sr., commander of the Stephen's Creek Regiment and several companies of the Dutch Fork Regiment; Maj. Patrick Cunningham, commander of the Little River Regiment and several companies of the Dutch Fork Regiment. Col. Vezey Husbands was present also, but it is unclear as to which unit he led. He was from Burke County, so he had probably just joined Ferguson's Corps about a week before the battle.

Many of the Tory militiamen were kith and kin, with at least eighteen sets of fathers and sons and forty-two sets of brothers. These combinations provided a tally of at least 170 family members stationed upon King's Mountain. Among the loyalists assembled under Ferguson's command, the Cunningham family was apparently the largest contributor of men from a single family. In addition to Capt. "Bloody Bill" Cunningham and Maj. Patrick Cunningham, there were at least five other men from that family on King's Mountain. There were numerous sets of cousins, and several men were related to members of their approaching enemies. Highlighting the passionate differences that divided these families, the Goforth family of Tryon (now Rutherford) County had three brothers in Ferguson's Corps and, unbeknownst to them, their other two brothers, both devout Patriots, were marching towards them.

Within the ranks of the Loyalist militia, their trihorn hats were graced with cockades fashioned of evergreen. While the militia did not have uniforms, the British army had equipped their officers with swords and the enlisted men were armed with "Brown Bess" muskets. However, most of their muskets were not equipped with bayonets, so Ferguson, the clever designer, adapted long knives to improvise as bayonets. With whittled handles, the loyalists' makeshift bayonets were crude and awkward; yet secured within the muzzle of their Brown Bess, these blades were capable of inflicting serious wounds. The British army placed a heavy emphasis on bayonet assaults, and Ferguson had trained his militia accordingly in "the spirit of the bayonet." His militia units mirrored British organizational structure, complete with companies and regiments commanded by officers, and their formations, movements, and tactics were well rehearsed.

Typical trihorn hat worn by American and British soldiers

Around 2:45 P.M., Major Winston's party approached what he believed was King's Mountain. At the base of the heights in his assigned sector of the northeast corner, his men dismounted and stealthily crept upward toward the crest. As they neared their objective, several unnamed compatriots (probably Campbell's men) approached them with the news that they were on the wrong precipice and redirected them. It is most probable that Winston had swung too far to the southwest and as he approached the chain of heights before him (known today as Brushy Ridge), he simply selected the wrong mountain. Their actual objective was still a good 2,400 to 3,000 feet before them, so Winston ordered his men to remount and off they rode. Realizing the importance of their grievous error, Winston's party rode, in the words of historian Lyman Draper, "like so many fox hunters, at an almost break-neck speed, through rough woods and brambles, leaping branches and crossing ridges."

As with any military operation, the best of plans are often affected by a myriad of unforeseen situations and the Patriot partisans at King's Mountain were no exception. On the north side of the mountain, the bulk of the Patriot "Left Division" was bogged down in marshy terrain several hundred yards from their objective. The area they traversed is dominated by a large draw that provides natural drainage from the surrounding heights. Within this draw, at the base of King's Mountain, the headwaters of several streams and a natural spring combined, forming a creek that drained the surrounding elevations and the northern slopes of King's Mountain.

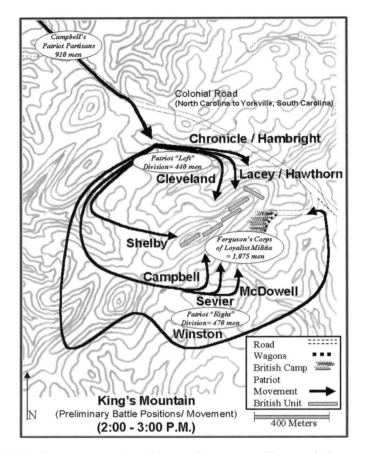

With the recent rains, the creek was swollen and the surrounding area was turned into a giant morass of mush and thick underbrush. The Patriots did their best to wade through quickly, but quietly. The only Patriot unit on the north side of the mountain (Left Division) moving at good speed and unimpeded was Shelby's column. His route to the objective was dominated by high ground and easily traversed. As Shelby's men approached their assault positions, beyond them to the southwest, Campbell's column was making its curve around the end of the mountain and getting very close to their own launch positions. In accordance with their plan, trailing behind Campbell's force, Sevier and McDowell's men would follow suit, continuing around the southern flank of the mountain and extending their lines toward the northeast.

At approximately 2:55 P.M., on the northern slope of the southwest end of the mountain, Loyalist security forces detected movement in the woods before them. At this same instant on the mountain precipice above, Adjutant Chesney was, according to his account, in the process of reporting to Major Ferguson that there were no signs of rebels in the area and "that all was quiet and the pickets on the alert." Then, Chesney said, "we heard their firing" which he thought was on the pickets. While the gunfire Chesney heard was not coming from the enemy, the solitude on King's Mountain was ended. Loyalist pickets began a sporadic fire aimed at Shelby's column moving below them. Yet, while the Patriots had lost their advantage of surprise, the fire from the nervous sentries created little more than an annoyance for the Patriots, and they continued moving into position. Within Shelby's ranks, the mountain men expressed an eagerness to return fire, but Shelby had always taught them to "Never shoot until you see an enemy, and never see an enemy, without bringing him down." Shelby, the experienced leader, demanded discipline, and he exclaimed to his men, "press on to your places, and then your fire will not be lost." Shortly after the fire began on Shelby's column, the other northern columns of the "Left Division" met pickets at the base of the northeast sector of the mountain and sporadic fire started there as well. On the summit, Ferguson strained to assess the situation, while his adjutant, Chesney, "immediately paraded the men and posted the officers."

Amidst the beating of the British drums, Ferguson's whistle shrieked its audible commands and his Loyalist militia went to work. Major Ferguson accompanied Captain DePeyster and his "Provincial Rangers" to the southwest corner of the ridge to counter the initial threat.

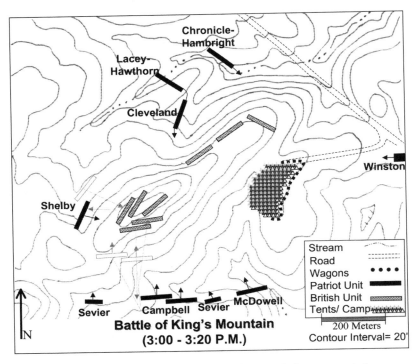

Battle of King's Mountain
(3:00 - 3:20 P.M.)

Moving around the southwest base of the mountain, one of Campbell's scouts, Phillip Grier, was seen by the Tory sentries and he was forced to shoot in self-defense. Ferguson's forces were now well aware of the Patriots' arrival. Peering below, along the base of King's Mountain, Ferguson could see movement, but not yet enough to get a definitive view of his enemy's intent. Campbell, realizing that the Left Division in the north as well as his own forces on the right were compromised, suddenly made a command decision to assault the heights. Campbell ordered his column to halt, dismount, and form units for the attack. He then dispatched a detachment of mounted troops, commanded by Capt. Andrew Colville, to attack a heavily manned enemy position that could be seen about halfway up the mountain. As the main force prepared for the ascent on foot, Colville's cavalry force rushed upward towards their foe. Simultaneously, Colonel Campbell threw off his coat and yelled as loud as he could, "Here they are my brave boys; shout like hell and fight like devils." Campbell's call for action was immediately followed by an uproar of shrill Indian war whoops that reverberated throughout the forest. With at least 910 Patriot voices screaming madly below, there was little doubt in the Loyalist ranks above that the battle of King's Mountain was under way.

Ferguson's surgeon, Dr. Uzal Johnson (1757–1827), carried one of the few timepieces on the mountain and he noted the hour when the battle began as 3 P.M. Captain DePeyster remembered hearing the same devilish screams at the Battle of Musgrove's Mill and they concerned him. Striving to surmount the noise from below, DePeyster turned to Major Ferguson and shouted, "These things are ominous—these are the damned yelling boys!" In unison with the Indian war whoops, the mountain erupted with the thunder of arms, and the gut-wrenching screams of human agony. Captain Colville's mounted force smashed into the British lines about halfway up the mountain and, being unable to break through the line, they retreated below. As Colville's bloodied detachment rejoined with Campbell, who was leading the dismounted charge up the slope, the reactions to their first casualties were emotional. Included among the dead were two Virginians, Lt. Robert Edmondson Sr. and Ensign John Beattie. Watching helplessly below were Beattie's two brothers and the two sons of Robert Edmondson Sr. With tearful eyes and vengeful hearts, brothers, sons, and friends of the fallen Patriots all rushed headlong into the deadly fire of the British lines above them.

Since the attack had begun prematurely, Sevier's unit, traveling in the column behind Campbell's men, became intermingled and joined in the assault in the southwest end of the mountain. As described by Colonel Shelby:

The battle here became furious and bloody, and many that belonged to Sevier's column were drawn

Major Joseph McDowell

into the action at this point, to support their comrades . . . the men of my column, of Campbell's column, and a great part of Sevier's, were mingled together in the confusion of the battle.

Sevier's 120-man force retained some companies deployed into their assigned sector towards the northeast on Campbell's right, but he also had a large contingent assault the mountain between Campbell and Shelby's forces. This element drove upwards and directly onto the end of the ridge in the southwest corner of the mountain. Campbell had not fully extended his Right Division along the southern base of the mountain to the northeast as planned, so McDowell desperately urged his men to maneuver around Campbell's right. Eventually, McDowell did reach his assigned position, but in the meantime, some of his men made the assault intermingled with Campbell's force. Thus, for the first twenty minutes of the battle, the entire Right Division of the Patriot army bore the full brunt of the battle, as the other units had still not achieved their assigned positions to begin the assault.

Just as the battle began, Major Winston's party arrived in his assigned sector, and the other elements slowly moved into position during the time Campbell's mix of Virginians and North Carolinians faced off with Ferguson's finest forces in the southwest end of the mountain. In addition to DePeyster's Provincial Rangers, the Loyalist militia in the southwest sector were the experienced men from District Ninety-Six, South Carolinians who Ferguson had initially formed months before. They were well prepared for battle and Ferguson employed them skillfully.

As Campbell's Right Division neared the crest, Ferguson's whistle rose above the din, announcing the first of many bayonet charges. Leading the Loyalists in their bloody work were the red-coated Provincial Rangers. As the massive British wave of glistening bayonets rushed downhill into the Patriots below, the impact was severe and sent the Patriots reeling. Amongst the ranks of the British footmen rode officers wielding swords. These swift-moving mounts topped by skillful swordsmen easily cut down their retreating foe. Lt. Anthony Allaire of the Provincial Rangers "overtook an officer of the mountaineers, fully six feet high; and the British Lieutenant being mounted, dashed up beside his adversary, and killed him with a single blow of his sword." As Campbell's men retreated down the slopes, many took shelter behind rocks and trees, remaining hidden until the British lines returned to the crest. At the bottom of the mountain, Campbell and his officers rallied their men and urged them back up the summit. As the main force passed by Robert Edmondson Jr., he, although badly wounded in the arm, stated, "Let us at it again," and they all repeated their assault up the mountain. Campbell's forces were again repelled at the point of bayonets, and their casualties were mounting. Again they rallied together and they repeated their efforts to dislodge the British from the heights above them. In the third and final bayonet assault, Captain DePeyster stated that the Patriots were nearly routed, and many of them fled beyond the base of the mountain.

According to DePeyster, "Unfortunately Major Ferguson made a signal for us to retreat, being afraid that the enemy would get possession of the height from the other side." When Ferguson blew his whistle and recalled the Provincial Rangers, to the summit, the South Carolina Loyalist militia that accompanied DePeyster's charge became confused.

This confusion of the Loyalist militia, coupled with the threat emanating from the opposite flank, provided the Patriots with a glimmer of hope. Campbell and his officers desperately yelled for their men to return. According to Lt. Samuel Newell, after bearing the British charge, the Virginians "broke and fled down the mountain—further indeed than necessary." Had Campbell's main force and initial attack been repelled or defeated, the battle might have ended right there. Yet, Campbell's men had been saved by their friends and neighbors led by Isaac Shelby. The repeated British assaults delivered in the southwest provided enough relief on the northwest slope for Shelby's men to gain ground. Yet, just as Shelby's force neared the summit in their sector of assault, Ferguson dispatched his bayonet-wielding forces into the ranks of those mountaineers. Shelby's men were also driven down to the base of the mountain, and thus far Ferguson's brash statement that "all the rebels in hell could not push him off" remained true.

Back at the base of the mountain, Shelby rallied his men and exclaimed, "Now boys, quickly reload your rifles, and let's advance upon them, and give them another hell of fire!" Shelby's men repeated their assault, and yet again, they were sent reeling downward. As the mountain men absorbed the shocks of the bayonet assaults and returned to the mountain, their unit formations broke into pockets of small teams and individual assaults, which created a swarming effect. The same thing occurred throughout the ranks of the Patriot units; as Cleveland stated to his men before the fight, each man had to be his own commander "and act on his own judgment." This actually worked in

Engraving of The Battle of King's Mountain

favor of the partisan Patriots, who excelled in working up
the mountain in small pockets of men supporting one
another as they moved. Like Indians, the Patriot mountain
men incessantly pressed toward the summit and amidst the
smoke and confusion, their enemy could not determine
where to focus next. One of Shelby's men, Josiah Culbertson,
a well-known marksman, worked his way towards an ele-
vated position where he worked as a sniper, shooting Tory
leaders in the head. This type of work was precisely what
the Patriots needed to dislodge their adversaries from the
heights and they poured it on.

As Campbell's, Sevier's, and Shelby's men pressed into
the British lines near the southwestern tip of the summit,
the battle turned into a hand-to-hand struggle. Men tore at
one another in fierce and imprudent rages. One was Capt.
William Edmondson. With several members of his family
killed and wounded, Edmondson rushed crazily into the
Provincial Rangers, shooting, clubbing, and slicing his way
through their ranks. He then resorted to his fists, beating
and clawing at them. In the midst of his rage, he clutched
one of the Redcoats by the neck and dragged him down the

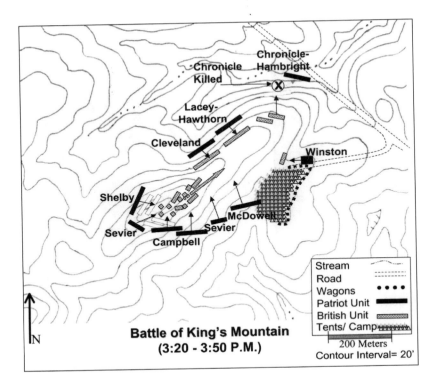

Battle of King's Mountain
(3:20 - 3:50 P.M.)

Stream
Road
Wagons
Patriot Unit
British Unit
Tents/ Camp
200 Meters
Contour Interval= 20'

mountain while tearing at his throat and beating him senseless. When Edmondson finished his foe, he charged back to the summit where he returned to the fray. At some point in the ensuing melee, Edmondson's adversaries shot him and he fell mortally wounded.

Meanwhile, in Ferguson's rear, the heights in the northeast were soon threatened by the arrival of the other Patriots. Ferguson ordered Captain DePeyster and his men down to the northeast crest to assist in that section, leaving the Loyalist militia to defend the heights from the "Overmountain Men." Ferguson then rode down the ridge to provide his personal leadership in that area, which was being assaulted by Majors Winston and Chronicle in the northeast and by Colonels Cleveland, Williams and Lacey along the northern slopes. The units attacking along the northern slopes faced difficult terrain, as the elevation was steeper and the vegetation denser than along the opposite flank.

At approximately 3:30 P.M., in the extreme northeast corner, the other Patriots of the Left Division made it into their respective assault positions. Already exhausted from their grueling movement through the swampy lowland and from fighting the British sentries at the base of the northern slopes, they formed into position while under fire from the British on the high ground above them. Major Chronicle and Lieutenant Colonel Hambright's "South Fork boys" formed in front of the steep heights at the extreme northeastern corner of the mountain and, led by Chronicle, they began the assault in that sector.

Chronicle stepped out in front of his ranks, raised his hat, and yelled for his men to "Face to the Hill!" As the formation began its movement, a heavy volley of British fire instantly killed William Chronicle and his boyhood friend William Rabb. According to Pvt. James Collins, "The shot of the enemy soon began to pass over us like hail. The first shock was quickly over, and for my own part, I was soon in a profuse sweat." Although badly shaken, the "South Fork boys" reformed their lines with Hambright in command. Struggling to take the heights, the men clambered over the craggy rock-strewn slopes as the British poured volleys of deadly fire into them. To their right, the units of Colonels Cleveland, Williams, and Lacey had begun their ascent of the heights as well. Above them, strewn along the brow of the northern ridge, the British forces poured a heavy hail of fire down below.

Throughout the ascent, Colonel Cleveland inspired his men by yelling words of encouragement, such as "Yonder is your enemy and the enemy of mankind!" and "A little nearer to them, my brave men!" Cleveland was an experienced commander and attempted to maintain unit integrity during the assault. Yet, as happened on the other end of the mountain, the inherent difficulty of climbing

Engraving taken from Lyman Draper's book on King's Mountain depicting the battle

and fighting forced the Patriots to disperse. At least they continued the fight.

On the summit above them, DePeyster's Provincial Rangers readied themselves for a bayonet charge. The focus was Hambright's men, who were struggling upward in the extreme northeast slope. In this area the slope was steep and the ensuing charge of the Loyalist bayonets came swiftly and with great force. One of Hambright's "men" was fifteen-year-old Robert Henry, who was busy reloading his rifle as the British with their deadly sharpened steel charged toward him. Just as young Henry was leveling his rifle, one of the British bayonets glanced off his rifle barrel "passing clear through one of his hands, and penetrating into his thigh." Henry managed to shoot his antagonist as they fell, and, locked in unison, tumbled down the hill. Henry's fire at point-blank range killed the British soldier, who was bleeding profusely as Henry writhed in pain and fought the shock of the incident. From his vantage point on the ground, young Henry observed his fellow South Fork boys discharge their rifles with deadly effect into the charging Britons, who then withdrew back up the mountain. Covering the withdrawal of the Provincial Rangers, the Loyalist militia above poured a maelstrom of lead down below. William Caldwell saw his bleeding young friend, Henry, lying on the ground and rushed to his aid. Caldwell pulled the bayonet from Henry's thigh, but he could not pry it from his friend's hand, so he quickly kicked the hand with the protruding bayonet and pulled Henry to safety.

Unbeknownst to the Patriots fighting in the northern Left Division, their enemies above them were comprised primarily of North Carolinian Tories. This twist of fate resulted in North Carolina neighbors and kinsmen fighting directly against one another. One of the South Fork boys, William Twitty, witnessed the death of his best friend, and he also noted the smoke whence the fateful shot had sped. Filled with hatred, Twitty watched the location intently as a head eventually peered up from beneath the undergrowth. Twitty took aim, discharged a soldier's justice, and dropped his foe. Passing over the body later in the battle, Twitty discovered that his target was a despicable Tory from his neighborhood and the shot had blown out the Tory's brains. In another incident, Patriot Maj. Thomas Young recorded that in his unit he paired off with one of his men and:

> Ben Hollingsworth and I took right up the side of the mountain and fought our way from tree to tree, up to the summit. I recollect I stood behind one tree, and fired until the bark was nearly all knocked off, and my eyes were pretty well filled with it. One fellow shaved me pretty close, for his bullet took a piece out of my gunstock. Before I was aware of it, I found myself apparently between my own regiment and the enemy, as I judged from seeing the paper which the Whigs wore in their hats, and the pine twigs the Tories wore in theirs, these being the badges of distinction.

As Young made his way into the Loyalist lines near the crest of the mountain, suddenly one of the Loyalists threw down his weapon, ran toward Young, and embraced him with joy. The Loyalist soldier was Matthew McCrary, Young's cousin. According to Young, "I told him to get a gun and fight; he said he could not; when I bade him let me go, that I might fight."

Apparently in Cleveland's sector, the Loyalists made only one other bayonet charge down the northern slope. While the bloody work of the British bayonet charges was efficient, the Patriots remained committed to their assault. Cleveland's command pressed forward despite receiving a number of casualties, many of whom were key leaders. Three brothers of the Lewis family, Maj. Micajah Lewis, Capt. Joel Lewis, and Lt. James Lewis, received a total of six horrible wounds, but, much to their mother's delight, all three survived. John Fields was stabbed three times, twice in the legs and once in the left breast, but he too survived. Colonel Cleveland lost several horses cut from beneath him, and, like his fellow Patriot officers, he wisely continued the fight on foot. As his men reeled from the point of the bayonet, they faced an unending hail of fire from above them. Another member of Cleveland's command, Capt. William Lenoir, while ascending the heights, was shot in the side. Then, he wheeled and was shot in the left arm and, in his own words, "after that, a bullet went through my hair above where it was tied, and my clothes were cut in several places."

While the Left Division tried valiantly to gain the heights in its sector, the terrain was steep and with the fire pouring down from above, the men were not able to take the heights. Still, their constant pressure forced Ferguson to direct resources to the northeast, thus providing some relief on the opposite slopes. With the Patriots crushing inward from all sides, the pressure cracked the Loyalists' lines, and their strength to defend the heights eroded. In the southwest corner of the mountain, the Patriot Right Division began pushing the Loyalist militia from its strongholds in

"The Battle of King's Mountain" by South Carolina artist Robert Wilson

the rocky heights. As Campbell's men clambered across the summit, one severely wounded South Carolinian Tory, Drury Mathis, played dead. He survived and later recorded his observations of the triumphant mountain men. Mathis refers to them as the "devils from the infernal regions" and he describes them as the most awesome warriors he had ever seen, "tall, raw-boned, sinewy, with long matted hair." As the mountaineers passed over his seemingly dead body, Mathis states that they were "so full of excitement" and "they darted like enraged lions up the mountain." The victors may have seemed larger than life from Mathis's position on the ground, but the Patriots were utterly exhausted. With the Loyalists surrendering their positions, the mountain men poured onto the summit of the ridge and the tide of battle began to turn. On the summit, Shelby, Sevier, and Campbell rallied their men.

After catching their breath and reforming into a semblance of unity, they all pressed forward. With the Left Division mounting the crest in their sector, and the Right Division's triumph in the southwest, Campbell ran atop a mass of rocks and peered down to the northeast. Campbell could clearly see that on both flanks and in the rear, the Patriots were

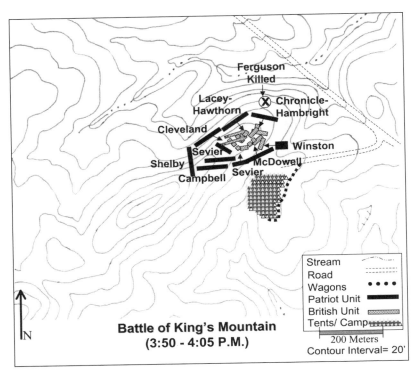

**Battle of King's Mountain
(3:50 - 4:05 P.M.)**

Stream
Road
Wagons
Patriot Unit
British Unit
Tents/ Camp

200 Meters
Contour Interval= 20'

meeting with success. Eager to continue their momentum, Campbell ran to the front of his mountaineers and yelled, "Boys, remember your liberty! Come on! Come on my brave fellows; another gun—another gun will do it! Damn them, we must have them out of this!" The Patriots then renewed their attack and zealously continued the fight.

While the Patriots in the northeast sector failed to take the heights, they maintained their position and Ferguson's Corps was trapped. Pressed into an ever-constricting mass, surrounded by his enemy, and ensnared within an enclave at the northeast end of the mountain, Ferguson had few options. He was restrained within his own formations, tents, and wagons, and he had no room to maneuver, but Ferguson was a warrior and surrender was not an option. Like a wildcat backed into a corner, Ferguson suddenly lashed out at his enemy with a lethal counterattack. Yet again, Ferguson sounded the assault with his silver whistle, and he sent DePeyster's Provincial Rangers to face the mountaineers swarming down upon them along the ridge from the southwest. Ferguson also ordered a mounted force of twenty Provincial Rangers led by Lt. John Taylor to charge into the approaching horde of Patriots.

DePeyster's Rangers were soon firing well-aimed volleys into the approaching mountain men, but Taylor's cavalrymen were picked off rapidly by the backwoods sharpshooters. Colonel Shelby, at the front of the Patriot formation, was nearly killed when a British musket discharged directly alongside the left side of his face. While the exploding gases at the end of the barrel scorched off the hair on the left side of his head, the deadly lead shot intended for Shelby's skull passed harmlessly beyond him. Stunned, burned, and somewhat deafened by the incident, Colonel Shelby was a lucky man, and he continued the fight.

Pressing forward, the swarming Patriots soon gained the upper hand, as they picked off Tories in the open plateau before them. The Patriots focused on DePeyster's Redcoats and within a matter of minutes the accurate fire of the backwoodsmen had decimated them. The demise of the Provincial Rangers spelled doom for the remainder of Ferguson's demoralized army. Ferguson struggled to rally his forces, but they were running out of ammunition. Amidst the smoke, noise, and confusion, the battle reached its violent crescendo. By one account, several Tories began to wave white handkerchiefs in an effort to surrender. Ferguson, wearing his checkered hunting shirt or duster, was clearly seen cutting these men down, and then dashing into the enemy lines slashing at Patriots until his sword was broken. Ferguson then organized a hasty assault force consisting of himself, two mounted Tory officers, and a dozen Loyalist foot soldiers with primed muskets. Mounted on his large white stallion, Ferguson took the lead and ordered a charge directly into Sevier's approaching ranks.

The dashing Scotsman was plainly visible to everyone around him, including several of Sevier's sharpshooters, John Gilleland, John Kusick, and Robert Young. Undoubtedly there were others with Ferguson in their sights, but according to these men, Gilleland yelled to Young, "There's Ferguson—shoot him!"

"I'll try and see what 'Sweet Lips' can do," muttered Young, as he drew a sharp sight, discharging his rifle, when Ferguson fell from his horse.

As Ferguson fell from his horse, he was pierced by at least six well-aimed and close range shots. One of the large-caliber rounds was driven into his face, several others entered his torso, and his limbs were bloodied. His frightened horse paraded Ferguson's shattered body around the mountain for several minutes, since a foot remained caught in the stirrup. Ferguson's orderly, Elias Powell, and several of his comrades hurriedly retrieved their commander and carried him away from the field of battle. In the same volley that struck Ferguson, Sevier's men also felled his accompanying officers, Loyalist Col. Vezey Husbands and Maj. Daniel Plummer. Husbands was killed, and Plummer was horribly wounded (left for dead, but he recovered).

Capt. Abraham DePeyster assumed command of the remnants of Ferguson's shattered army. As described by the Loyalist surgeon, Dr. Uzal Johnson:

> DePeyster then gave the word to form and charge. The cry throughout the militia line was "we are out of ammunition," this being our unhappy condition, and the militia (though they stood and fought bravely while their ammunition lasted) were now getting the utmost disorder. It was thought most expedient to send out a (surrender) flag to save a few brave men that survived the heat of action.

Colonel Campbell's younger cousin, Ensign Robert Campbell, noted that "Captain DePeyster raised a flag, and

Major Samuel Hammond

called for quarters; it was soon taken out of his hand by one of the officers on horseback, and raised so high that it could be seen by our line." Although surrender flags were being waved, some Loyalists continued to fight and the battle, although subsiding, continued producing casualties.

In its final moments, amidst the confusion, the ensuing close-quarter battle created a hail of wild bullets throughout the heights, and many people were senselessly killed. At some point in the attack, one of the women in Ferguson's entourage, Virginia Sal, was killed by a random bullet. Among the Patriots killed during the closing scenes of the battle was Colonel Williams. Riding towards the encircled enemy, suddenly Williams reeled in the saddle. According to Patriot Thomas Young, "his horse was shot under the jaw, when he commenced stamping as if he were in a nest of yellow jackets." Williams released the reins, jumped off the wounded beast, and then he too was shot and mortally wounded. His men carried him into a nearby British tent, where his sons tried desperately to help their

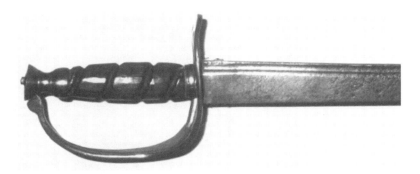

Colonel Frederick Hambright's sword

father. Yet, Williams faced his fate and stated, "I am a gone man." Maj. Samuel Hammond took William's command and the unfortunate Patriot urged the men onward with, "For God's sake, boys, don't give up the hill!" Ferguson's adjutant, who was fighting alongside his commander, stated that it was Ferguson himself who fired the shots at Williams, whom Ferguson thought was the Patriot commander. Several Patriots collaborate Chesney's report, but we may never know for certain. About the same time, Lieutenant Colonel Hambright was also wounded. Despite suffering a severed leg artery that filled his boot with blood, Hambright remained in the saddle and he miraculously survived.

As the Patriots closed with the mass of Loyalist militia now herded into a draw at the northeast corner of the mountain, their passions overwhelmed their judgment and the killing continued. According to Colonel Shelby's younger brother, Evan Shelby Jr., "Our men who had been scattered in the battle were continually coming up, and continued to fire, without comprehending, in the heat of the moment, what had happened." Yet, despite the fact that the Loyalists were attempting to surrender, many Patriots called out for "Tarleton's quarter!" The phrase was echoed throughout the ridge, and bloody vengeance reigned. Even Colonel Campbell, having witnessed the shots that killed

Williams, ordered his men to fire into the horde of Loyalists huddled before them, which the Patriots did. Rumors circulated that Colonel Sevier had been killed. When his son, eighteen-year-old Joseph Sevier, heard this, he became embroiled with rage and started shooting into the Loyalists. Sobbing profusely, he cried out, "The damned rascals have killed my father, and I'll keep loading and shooting till I kill every son of a bitch of them." Sevier's embittered work did not end until his father rode up and informed his son that the rumor concerned not him, but the young lad's uncle, Robert Sevier, who was mortally wounded.

With the Patriots still firing into the defeated crowd, the Tories cried out for "Quarters, quarters!" Yet, the Tories retained their arms and many attempted to defend themselves. Colonel Shelby rode directly between the Tories and Patriots exclaiming, "Damn you, if you want quarters, throw down your arms!" Finally, Colonel Campbell realized his error, and he ran forward, knocking a rifle upwards that was being leveled at the Tories below. Campbell yelled at the perpetrator, Pvt. Andrew Evans, "Evans, for God's sake, don't shoot! It is murder to kill them now, for they have raised a flag!" Continuing his efforts to quell the senseless violence, Campbell rushed amongst his men yelling, "Cease firing!—For God's sake, cease firing!" With his fellow Patriot officers making similar pleas, the mad onslaught was quelled.

In a flurry of submissive gestures, the Loyalist officers surrendered their swords to whoever appeared to be a ranking Patriot. The Loyalists' commander, Capt. Abraham DePeyster, prematurely and inadvertently surrendered the British flag and his sword to the wrong man, Maj. Evan Shelby Jr. Campbell then approached Captain DePeyster, received the formal surrender, and ordered him to dismount. Campbell then shouted to the Tories, "Officers, rank by yourselves; prisoners, take off your hats and sit down." One of Campbell's men, Henry Dickenson, recorded that at

Captain Abraham DePeyster's sword; courtesy of the Tennessee State Museum

first, the Loyalist officers were hesitant towards Campbell's authority. Apparently, Campbell's haggard, battle-worn appearance did not meet the Loyalist expectations of a victorious field commander. Dickenson stated that in response to the actions of the Loyalist officers, "I took my gun from my shoulder, at the same time mentioning that this was our commander. The officers then bowed to Col. Campbell, and delivered their swords to him." Campbell then ordered the Loyalist officers to follow him, and he ordered his own men to form four concentric circles around the mass of Tory prisoners. DePeyster, who was naturally upset about the slaughter that occurred after raising the white flag, chastised the victorious commander with, "Colonel Campbell, It was damned unfair, it was damned unfair!" Be that as it may, Campbell was in no mood to mince words with an adversary who was now his prisoner. Once the Loyalists were securely disarmed, segregated, and well-guarded,

Campbell led his men in shouting three times, "Hurrah for liberty!"

Reveling in victory, the Patriots shouted and hugged one another with great glee. Emotions ran amok as their eyes searched for their friends and family. When Colonel Sevier saw his friend Colonel Shelby, he pointed to his head wound and shouted, "By God, they've burned off your hair!" As the victory stomp ended, the shouts of joy were replaced by the incessant moaning of the wounded and dying, which lay all around them. According to Doctor Johnson, the battle had lasted sixty-five minutes, and in that time at least 500 casualties spilled their blood upon King's Mountain. Fully one-third of the battle's participants were now lying on the ground, and most of them were dead. A young Patriot survivor, James Collins, described the scene:

> After the fight was over, the situation of the poor Tories appeared to be really pitiable; the dead lay in heaps on all sides, while the groans of the wounded were heard in every direction. I could not help turning away from the scene before me, with horror, and though exulting in victory, could not refrain from shedding tears.

The "groans of the wounded" numbered 221, while the number of doctors available to help them was just one. The duty of salvaging lives depended solely upon the gifted hands of Doctor Johnson, the only surviving surgeon on the mountain (two others died in battle). This intrepid surgeon was undoubtedly assisted in such an ominous task by assistants with experience in the art of healing. While these hardy people of rural eighteenth-century America were well accustomed to treating their own wounds, success was often illusive. Johnson was an experienced battlefield surgeon and records indicate that several amputees and gunshot victims owed their lives to his professional skills. While there are conflicting reports concerning the precise casualty figures, the following table reflects the author's conservative analysis, and the reports of Doctor Johnson and Colonel Campbell:

	KIA	WIA	WIA (Mortally)	Comments
Patriots	29	58	4	Recorded in a by-name list
Loyalists	244	163	?	Includes Provincial Rangers
British	1	-	-	Major Patrick Ferguson
Civilian	1	-	-	Virginia Sal
TOTAL	275	221	4	500—Total Casualties

As with any battle, the sheer number of casualties reflects the horrors of war, but this battle was especially abhorrent due to the composition of its combatants and their enflamed vehemence. While political ideology divided them between Whigs and Tories, their familial roots were deeply entwined. With the exception of Major Ferguson, all of the combatants were Americans, and in most cases, their families were but one generation removed from a shared heritage in Great Britain. Nonetheless, on King's Mountain, hatred bitterly divided them, and for several families, the costs were incredibly high. With at least seventy-four sets of brothers and twenty-nine sets of fathers and sons committed in battle, tragic losses and heart-wrenching anguish were certainties.

Highlighting this situation is the Goforth family. Five Goforth brothers clashed in this battle and only one, John Goforth, a Patriot, survived. His brother Preston, a Patriot, and three brothers who were Tories all died on King's Mountain. Another family, the Mattocks, lost Patriot Capt. John Mattocks, and his brother Edward, a Tory, was horribly wounded. Four members of the Brandon family served the Patriot cause, while two of their kinsman were Tories. One of them, Capt. Thomas Brandon, was killed.

While there were other incidents such as these, the cross-combatant-line casualties pale in regard to those incurred by family members serving on the same side. Col. James Williams, who was mortally wounded near the end of the battle, was the father of two teen-age officers at King's Mountain, Joseph and Daniel. Within one year, in an act of retribution, William's two sons were executed by Tory "Bloody Bill" Cunningham. Cunningham's family had suffered casualties at King's Mountain too. Colonel Sevier lost his brother, Robert, and although Colonel Shelby's brother Moses was badly wounded, he survived. While Colonel Campbell had several kinsmen in his command, they all survived the battle. However, Campbell's regiment, which had borne the brunt of the battle, suffered the heaviest casualties. Fully one-third of the Patriot casualties were members of Campbell's command, including thirteen officers. One of these officers was Ens. John Beattie, whose killing early in the battle was witnessed by his two brothers. Shortly after the battle, in a letter to his family, Campbell stated, "I have lost several of my good friends, whose death I much lament." Campbell's letter went on to highlight four casualties incurred by the Edmondsons, to whom his family was very close. Three brothers in the Edmondson family, William, Robert Sr., and Andrew, were all killed, while Robert Jr., although badly wounded, survived. Campbell and William Edmondson had served during the Indian wars together and they were both founding fathers of the town of Abingdon, Virginia.

While there were numerous casualties and families on both sides of the battle were deeply affected, the sole Briton on King's Mountain was Maj. Patrick Ferguson. His life presents us with a man whose notoriety and brash statements made his death the climax of the battle. Besides, by issuing an ultimatum to a proud people seeking freedom from tyranny and despotism, Ferguson made himself the target of their frustration. Through his words and deeds, Ferguson became the embodiment of everything the American Patriots abhorred. In his life, the Patriots saw an illusive and oppressive evil, and in his death, the Patriots saw hope and freedom. Ultimately, Ferguson's demise did mark a turn of events in the Patriots' favor; therefore, his death and what happened to him afterward have been the topic of great speculation. There are several accounts of his demise and they are laced with obvious fiction and irrelevant material. However, though Ferguson was a colorful character and a proud soldier, ultimately he was flesh and blood. Ferguson readily succumbed to death in the form of numerous lead bullets that lacerated his body. The details concerning where and how many bullets made their mark are ultimately irrelevant. We do know that the victorious Patriots were anxious to view his mutilated corpse and many of them did so. We also know that the patriots (and several Tories) stripped his body and removed his earthly possessions. Various accounts also hint that the Patriots urinated on Ferguson's lifeless body. We will never know for certain. According to Powell when the Patriots brought Ferguson to the stream, he was still breathing. Again, this may be, but does it really matter? Perhaps Ferguson, was afforded a precious moment of solitude, before surrendering his body to the mountain he so fervently defended.

It could be argued that as a soldier Ferguson certainly deserved a respite. While we may disagree with Ferguson's commitment to king and country, one must admire his indomitable spirit. Within his letters, Ferguson revealed the personal traits of a true soldier. Writing home to his friends and family, Ferguson stated:

> I thank God more for this than for all his other blessings, that in every call of danger, or honor, I have felt myself collected and equal to the occasion . . . The length of our lives is not at our own command, however much the manner of them may be. If our creator enables us to act the part of men of honor, and to conduct ourselves with spirit, probity, and humanity, the change to another world, whether now, or fifty years hence, will not be for the worse.

One of Ferguson's Provincial Rangers, Lt. Anthony Allaire, maintained a diary throughout their campaign in the Carolinas. His entry on October 7, 1780, provides lamentations about their staggering defeat on King's Mountain, but it also includes a heartfelt eulogy of his fallen commander. Allaire recorded:

> We lost in this action, Maj. Ferguson, of the Seventy-first regiment, a man much attached to his King and country, well informed in the art of war; he was brave and humane, and an agreeable companion; in short, he was universally esteemed in the army, and I have every reason to regret his unhappy fate.

Elias Powell and his assistants washed Ferguson's body, wrapped it in a large leather hide, and buried his remains within a draw on the northeast end of the mountain. Stones were placed atop the grave as a marker and to discourage scavengers. Ultimately, Ferguson's declaration that "all the rebels in hell could not push him off" of King's Mountain held true. His body remains on the mountain.

The overwhelming victory achieved by the Patriots on King's Mountain is rare in the annals of warfare, but Ferguson made serious mistakes. While we do not know his precise reasons for choosing the mountain defense, obviously Ferguson saw merit in the position, and boasted of it. There was a plentiful supply of water nearby and he held the high ground, forcing his enemy to fight an uphill battle. But Ferguson may have found the heights most desirable because he knew the mountain defense would force his militia to fight for their lives: If they decided to run, they could not. Yet, in choosing to do battle on this mountain, he placed his army in a vulnerable position. Militarily, his position was weak, and military strategists have criticized what they say were Ferguson's miscalculations and inadequate preparations:

British Brown Bess Musket
.75 caliber, with bayonet

A 1780 military musket had a smoothbore .75 caliber barrel (inside diameter) that fired a .69 caliber lead ball. The loose-fitting ball bounced from side to side inside the barrel when fired, causing it to wobble in flight. This gave the musket an effective range of about 75 yards. A 16-inch triangular bayonet completed the weapon.

American Long Rifle
.50 caliber

Rifling, the spiral grooving within the length of a gun barrel, stabilized the lead ball in flight by forcing it to spin on its axis like a gyroscope. The long rifle's slender barrel (about 48 inches long with a .50 caliber bore) allowed the gunpowder to fully combust. This extra energy thrust the spinning ball faster and farther- up to 300 yards.

Typical rifles used by American and British troops

1. His enemy was afforded excellent concealment as they approached their objective.
2. Ferguson's army did not have clear fields of fire, and their position was too restrictive.
3. Once Ferguson was cornered at the top of the mountain, his enemy was afforded clear fields of fire.
4. While there were posted sentries, they were too close to the position being defended.
5. Ferguson did not send out roving mounted scouts, who could have provided warning hours before hand.

Complicating matters was the differences in arms and tactics. The Patriots' Long Rifles were much more accurate and had a greater range than the inferior British Brown Bess guns (although Ferguson had tried to correct that years before). Ferguson employed formations and drill maneuver in terrain unsuitable for such tactics. While Ferguson's men delivered deadly blows with their bayonets, the shock effect of these assaults subsided, as this tactic was designed for open terrain, and impractical in the forest. Once the backwoodsmen learned to deal with the bayonets, the tide of battle changed. The terrain on King's Mountain provided the advantage to the Patriots, who fought "Indian style," providing them with flexible maneuver, maximum use of cover and concealment, and swarming of the objective.

By all accounts, however, had the Patriots not been as zealous in their resolve, the battle could have easily gone the other way. At several points in the beginning of the fight, Ferguson nearly routed the Patriots. If some Patriots had fled in the early stages of the battle, their comrades would have probably followed suit. Ferguson was undoubtedly looking to exploit this frequent weakness in the Patriot army. But these men were a different breed than Ferguson normally dealt with. As DePeyster had warned his commander, "These things are ominous—these are the damned yelling boys!"

The patriot "yelling boys" and their triumphant battle at King's Mountain were indeed "ominous" for the British. The immediate thoughts of the victorious Patriots, however, focused on rest, relief, and recuperation. While their victory would ease the grip of British oppression at home, they had no idea how important their efforts would prove to be. On the eve of that victory as the sun ebbed in the western sky, British domination of the Carolinas waned too.

3

THE CONSEQUENCE OF VICTORY

THE DAWN AFTER THE BATTLE OF King's Mountain showed the promise of a beautiful day. Bathed in the warmth of the autumn sun, the weary survivors stretched, strained, and slowly urged their aching bodies back to life. Colonel Shelby recorded that on that morning he faced the sky "enjoying the warmth of the sun, for I had been very wet the day before, and was exposed to the cold dew of the mountain all night." Strewn about them, however, were the remains of several hundred shattered and bloody corpses. For Col. William Campbell, the word of the day was responsibility. Campbell was surrounded by hundreds of corpses (at least 277 in total—29 Patriots and 246 Loyalists), and he felt they should be afforded a decent burial. Campbell also had an estimated 800 prisoners (again, there are conflicting reports), and at least 163 of them were wounded. He also had 871 remaining of his own men and sixty-two of them were wounded. The only surgeon on the mountain, Dr. Uzal Johnson, had worked through the night and saved several lives. Overwhelmed with casualties, by candlelight he amputated limbs and treated gunshots as best as he could with nothing more than rum, rags, the crude tools of a field surgeon, and his own skills.

Campbell, the Patriot commander, faced myriad complications. Paramount was the threat of a British response. Campbell knew that the bulk of the British army was too close for comfort. Lord Cornwallis was nearby in Charlotte and the threat of Tarleton's dragoons was omnipresent. Additionally, Campbell's forces were hungry, exhausted, and burdened with a captive army as nearly as large as his own. Local civilians arrived in search of their loved ones, and upon viewing the carnage and many finding the gory remains of their relatives and friends, emotions were running very high. Campbell's primary concern was to leave King's Mountain as quickly as possible, yet there was a lot of work to be done. Wasting little time, he ordered several of the British wagons burned, as the Patriots did not need them. To evacuate the casualties, he had litters fashioned from blankets and poles and lashed to horses. To reduce the burden of hauling the 1,500 captured rifles, he issued one to each prisoner and they reluctantly carried them. Finally, before the long train of evacuees departed the heights, Campbell organized both Patriot and Tory burial parties to remain behind. The burials were hastily conducted by scraping out two long trenches in the rocky surface, and covering the dead with a thin layer of soil. The makeshift graves, dug without adequate tools or time, would yield their contents in the weeks ahead (devoured by wolves, vultures, and wild pigs, their bones "whitened" the mountain for decades thereafter). Yet, the weary survivors had done the best they could, and they joined their fellow travelers.

The victorious Patriots moved northward, toward the safety of the mountains, and away from the British army. Campbell's mounted forces were soon re-joined by the footmen and weaker horses that followed them from Cowpens. While this provided his warriors with some relief, the movement was burdened greatly by the prisoners, who were not eager to go anywhere. The journey was further complicated because the soldiers had little food, they were all exhausted, and Campbell (a Virginian) had no official command authority over the men from North Carolina. Furthermore, he was uncertain what to do with his prisoners. In a letter home, Campbell wrote, "I must proceed on with the prisoners until I can in some way dispose of them." Campbell dispatched swift-riding messengers to General Gates carrying news of the Patriot victory and requesting Gates's orders concerning the Tory prisoners.

As the Patriots traveled, they learned that many of their Tory prisoners had committed atrocities against their neighbors, and many called for immediate justice and retribution. Several prisoners were slaughtered on the spot by their accusers, and others were beaten and generally mistreated. Campbell ordered his officers to "exert themselves in suppressing this abominable practice, degrading to the name of soldier." Many Tories escaped or died trying, yet the bulk of them simply bore a very difficult and horrific journey. The Patriots herded their captives along and on October 13 they arrived at a local plantation, fifteen miles northeast of Gilbert Town. Here, the victors learned that numerous Patriots were recently hanged at Fort Ninety-Six. This news, combined with the passionate calls for justice from their men, convinced the Patriot commanders to conduct a trial.

Thus, in a virtually lawless land, amidst a violent revolution, the partisans found legal authority in North Carolina law to hold an ad hoc trial of men suspected of committing heinous crimes. That evening, at least thirty Tory prisoners were found guilty of "breaking open houses, killing the men, and turning the women and children out of doors and burning the houses." The next day, nine convicts were hanged. Undoubtedly, more would have met with the same fate, but the partisans were informed that Tarleton was hot on their trail. Finally, Campbell's messengers returned with word from Gates to deliver the prisoners to Hillsboro. The Patriots wasted no time as they collected their prisoners and continued the journey. Shortly thereafter, the partisan army disbanded and Col. Benjamin Cleveland was placed in charge of the prisoners. Colonel Sevier led the bulk of the "Overmountain Men" back into the Blue Ridge, and they

**Letter from General Gates concerning the disposition of
British prisoners; Library of Congress**

returned home. Colonels Campbell and Shelby rode on to
Gates's headquarters to make arrangements for the prisoners and to meet personally with the commanding general.

General Gates was the first Continental officer to formally
thank the partisan Patriots for their services rendered at
King's Mountain. Gates declared that the defeat of Ferguson
"gave me, and every friend to liberty, and the United States,

infinite satisfaction. I thank you gentlemen, and the brave officers and soldiers under your command, for your and their glorious behavior in that action." Unbeknownst to the victors of King's Mountain, their efforts had created an incredible turn of events, as the British campaign into North Carolina was reversed. Tarleton recorded in his memoirs:

> The destruction of Ferguson and his corps marked the period and the extent of the first expedition into North Carolina. Added to the depression and fear it communicated to the loyalists upon the borders, and to the southward, the effect of such an important event was sensibly felt by Earl Cornwallis at Charlotte town. The weakness of his army, the extent and poverty of North Carolina, the want of knowledge of his enemy's designs, and the total ruin of his militia, presented a gloomy prospect at the commencement of the campaign. A farther progress by the route, which he had undertaken could not possibly remove, but would undoubtedly increase his difficulties; he therefore formed a sudden determination to quit Charlotte town, and pass the Catawba River. The army was ordered to move, and expresses were dispatched to recall Lieutenant-Colonel Tarleton.

Cornwallis evacuated Charlotte and retreated sixty miles into South Carolina, where he established a defense at Winnsboro. He remained there throughout the winter, uncertain as to what he should do next. In District Ninety-Six, the British commander there, Colonel John Cruger, sent word that the Patriot victory at King's Mountain had reversed the loyalties of the locals. In fact, throughout the Carolinas, news of the overwhelming destruction of Ferguson's army, coupled with the retreat of Cornwallis, created a rally to the Patriot cause. Cornwallis tried to explain the defeat of Ferguson and his own situation to Sir Henry Clinton with:

The event proved unfortunate, without any fault of Major Ferguson's. A numerous and unexpected enemy came from the mountains; as they had good horses their movements were rapid. . . . After everything that has happened I will not presume to make your Excellency any sanguine promises.

When word of the unexpected Patriot victory at King's Mountain reached Gen. George Washington, the news probably seemed too good to be true. The battle was described as a "total defeat" of the British force commanded by Ferguson. Washington's formal announcement expressed some apprehension, yet within his concluding remarks, he also stated that the victory "will in all probability have a very happy influence upon the successive operations in that quarter." He continued, "It is proof of the spirit and resources of the country."

As expressed by Cornwallis and Washington, the Patriot victory at the battle of King's Mountain was certainly unexpected. Until that fateful day, the British army had easily dominated affairs throughout the southern states. Ultimately, the battle of King's Mountain served as the turning point in the Revolutionary War. In the words of Sir Henry Clinton, after this battle, the British campaign in the South took an unpromising turn "as a consequence of Maj. Ferguson's disaster and Lord Cornwallis's sudden retreat from Charlotte town, for a general panic and despondency appear to have immediately seized the militia and almost every other loyalist in the province." Clinton also stated that for the British, the loss at King's Mountain "unhappily proved the first link in a chain of events that followed each other in regular succession until they at last ended in the total loss of America."

From the Patriot perspective, as expressed by Thomas Jefferson, governor of Virginia, the victory "was the joyful annunciation of that turn in the tide of success that terminated the Revolutionary War with the seal of our Independence." While the reward of the Patriots' ser-

The official Declaration of the Patriot Victory at King's Mountain by the Continental Army

vices was ultimately freedom, none of them received any pay for their military services at King's Mountain. Congress publicly acknowledged their contributions and thanked them on November 13, as follows:

> Resolved, That Congress entertain a high sense of the spirited and military conduct of Colonel Campbell, and the officers, and privates of the Militia under his command, displayed in action of the 7 of October, in

which a complete victory was obtained over superior numbers of the enemy, advantageously posted on King's Mountain, in the state of North Carolina; and that this resolution be published by the commanding officer of the southern army, in general orders.

Years later, the states of Virginia and North Carolina awarded presentation swords to their respective commanders who served on King's Mountain. Additionally, once the United States achieved independence, the veterans of the Revolutionary War were rewarded with land grants and disability pensions, and in most cases, surviving widows were provided with a small pension. Members of the state militias, which included the partisan Patriots of King's Mountain, also qualified for these benefits. Many Patriot participants at King's Mountain continued selfless service to their nation, and some died fighting in other battles before the war was won. Some later served in public life as politicians and civic leaders during the initial growth of our new nation (see epilogue).

It was many years before the American public acknowledged the significance and the sanctity of the battlefield at King's Mountain. Due to its rural and isolated location, for years the only visitors to the battlefield were hunters, as the region was heavily populated with wolves. In 1815, a former Patriot surgeon, Dr. William McLean, led an effort to clean up the battleground. A commemorative ceremony was held on the anniversary of the battle, but first, the locals gathered the bones of fallen warriors that were strewn throughout the heights and reburied them. McLean and his associates then dedicated a monument to the combatants.

In 1855, nearly 55,000 people attended the seventy-fifth anniversary celebration of the battle, and in 1880, a twenty-eight-foot monument was unveiled during the battle's centennial celebration. Visitation to the battlefield waned until

1899, when the King's Mountain chapter of the Daughters of the American Revolution (DAR) initiated efforts to reclaim the battlefield from neglect. They also initiated a campaign for national recognition of the site and in 1909, the federal government erected a new eighty-three-foot U.S. monument. However, interest in the site was difficult to maintain. In 1930, during the celebration of the battle's sesquicentennial (150-year) anniversary, the keynote speech was delivered by President Herbert Hoover. The governors of both Carolinas were in attendance as well as 70,000 spectators and the national media. Hoover's speech was broadcast via radio throughout the United States and Great Britain. Hoover stated that at King's Mountain, "It was a little army and a little battle, but it was of mighty portent. History has done scant justice to its significance, which rightly should place it beside Lexington and Bunker Hill, Trenton, and Yorktown, as one of the crucial engagements in our long struggle for independence."

Today, the King's Mountain National Military Park is nestled within the larger protective reserve of King's Mountain State Park. Due to its isolation and efforts of the National Park Service, the area remains unmolested terrain. While it is readily accessible via modern roads, it lies within a rural and tranquil area that affords visitors a glimpse into the backwoods of the eighteenth century. Two large monuments dedicated in 1909 and 1930 to the "heroism and patriotism of the combatants" dominate the heights, while throughout the park several others honor individuals of the Patriot cause. The grave of Maj. Patrick Ferguson, considered by many as the most handsome marker on King's Mountain, is a solemn symbol that represents not only the death of a man, but the end of an era. His large cairn, built in the ancient Scottish tradition, serves as a reminder of our nation's European roots. His headstone, erected by the citizens of the United States, reflects America's admiration of a worthy foe. Below his name, it states:

A Soldier of Military
Distinction and of Honor

The Battle of King's Mountain was a dramatic and significant event in the history of these United States. While Ferguson's distinction and honor are exemplary in the annals of military history, so too are the efforts of those who opposed him. If not for the dedication, courage, and sacrifice of "a little army" of stubborn frontiersmen, the hope of freedom may have been vanquished forever.

Many of the men who fought at King's Mountain continued selfless service to their nation. Among these men, many sacrificed their lives before winning the freedom they so diligently fought to achieve. After the victory at King's Mountain, the surviving sons of Col. James Williams were pursued by "Bloody Bill" Cunningham, and in November 1781, after a battle at Haye's Station in South Carolina, they were captured by him. Capt. Daniel Williams (age eighteen) and his younger brother Joseph (age fourteen) were among thirteen men executed by Cunningham as a matter of retribution for King's Mountain. The elder brother, Daniel, was hanged alongside his commander, Colonel Joseph Hayes, both of whom were veterans of King's Mountain. Young Joseph watched in horror, as the men were hanged from a makeshift gallows. As they kicked and swung,, the pole snapped beneath their weight. Cunningham, ever true to his "Bloody Bill" sobriquet, hacked Hayes and both Williams brothers into small pieces with his sword.

The Patriot commander at King's Mountain, William Campbell, was another who never tasted the fruits of liberty. After the battle, he returned to his Virginia home in November 1780. However, in February 1781, Campbell reorganized his contingent of Washington County militia and they joined Gen. Nathaniel Greene's army in North Carolina. Cornwallis had finally launched his attack into North Carolina and he had issued an order that if

Campbell were caught, he would be hanged. Campbell responded with a similar threat directed at Cornwallis. Campbell's unit participated at the Battle of Guilford Courthouse in March, then they returned home, as Campbell resigned from the militia due to disagreements with Greene. Campbell was then elected to the Virginia House of Delegates, but after serving a short time, he rejoined the army after Cornwallis's army marched into the tidewater peninsula of Virginia. This time Campbell served as a brigadier general and he was assigned to the command of the Marquis de Lafayette. As the combined French and American forces pressed Cornwallis into his ultimate demise at the siege of Yorktown, General Campbell led a rifle unit. Yet, while serving in the field, Campbell was suddenly stricken with a "pain in the breast"—an apparent heart attack—and he died several days later, on August 22, 1781, two months before Cornwallis surrendered. Campbell was thirty-six years old. Lafayette, who had befriended Campbell, provided his eulogy and stated that Campbell's service to his country "endeared him to every citizen, and in particular to every American soldier." The marquis had him buried with military honors in the woods, west of Yorktown near Richmond; however, in 1823, his family had Campbell re-interred in the family cemetery at his beloved homestead in Aspenvale.

After King's Mountain, Lt. Col. John Sevier returned to fighting Indians, and he also served again in the revolution under the command of General Greene. He rose to the rank of brigadier general (militia) and after the war he began a career in politics. From 1789 to 1791, he served in the North Carolina legislature. He also led the endeavor to create the State of Franklin, in the region of what is now east Tennessee. While this initial movement to separate the area west of the Blue Ridge from North Carolina failed, ultimately Sevier's work in this area achieved success. The western hinterlands of North Carolina became the territory of Tennessee and Sevier returned to the militia as a brigadier general. After clearing the area of the Indian threat, in 1796, the state of Tennessee was organized from the western section of North Carolina, and Sevier was elected as its first governor. Sevier served as the governor and as a state senator until 1811, when he was elected to represent Tennessee in the U.S. Congress. Throughout the War of 1812, Congressman Sevier served on the Committee on Military Affairs. In 1815, President James Madison appointed Sevier a Commissioner of Indian Affairs on the frontier of the Creek nation. Sevier died while serving in this capacity at Fort Decatur, Alabama, on September 24, 1851. Reflecting a genuine affection for their native son, the people of Tennessee named a county and city in his honor.

Isaac Shelby, like his friend and neighbor John Sevier, returned home and engaged in frontier defense until General Greene requested that he assist the revolutionary cause once more. Shelby returned with his militiamen and again they rendered great service to their nation during the remainder of the Revolution. He then served as a member of the North Carolina Assembly and returned to militia service on the frontier. While performing his duties to clear the Kentucky region of Indians, he was instrumental in the creation of that territory as a state. Consequently, he became the first governor of Kentucky and he served several terms in that office, from 1792 to 1796 and again from 1812 to 1816. During the War of 1812, Shelby returned to military service and fought the British again in the Canadian campaign. In 1818, President James Monroe appointed Shelby Secretary of war, but Shelby declined, due to ill health. He did serve as an Indian commissioner with Gen. Andrew Jackson in the treaty negotiations for the lands west of Tennessee. During this service, Shelby had the first of several strokes. He suffered a general decline in his health and died on July 18, 1826. Like Sevier, Shelby is honored by Tennessee with both a county and city bearing his name.

Maj. Samuel Hammond, who, upon the death of Colonel Williams, took charge of the South Carolinians, continued his military service and rose to the rank of colonel. He fought at the battle of Cowpens and Guilford Courthouse. After the war, he moved to Georgia, which he represented in the U.S. Congress. He later returned to South Carolina, where he served as a legislator, surveyor general, and secretary of state. He died on September 11, 1843.

Several other Patriot commanders who served at King's Mountain continued to render public service to their nation. Among these men were: Col. Benjamin Cleveland, North Carolina congressman, senator, and judge (namesake of Cleveland County, North Carolina); Maj. Joseph Winston, congressman and state senator (namesake of Winston-Salem, North Carolina); Maj. Joseph McDowell, North Carolina congressman and senator; Maj. John Adair, congressman and governor of Kentucky as well as a general in the War of 1812; Maj. William Candler, Georgia congressman and judge; Col. Edward Lacey, brigadier general (militia), Kentucky legislator, and judge; Capt. John Brown, North Carolina congressman; and Capt. Jesse Hardin, congressman, senator, and governor of North Carolina.

While there were others whose services were no less valuable than the men mentioned above, these men and their contributions represented a slice of what General Washington referred to as the "spirit and resources of the country" with which independence was achieved and a new nation was founded.

The Loyalists who were defeated at the Battle of King's Mountain were also Americans. Some of these men converted to the Patriot cause and contributed to the birth of their nation. Ultimately, the Loyalist or Tory ideology was crushed by the formation of the United States and these people faced a difficult choice. While many of them embraced their new nation and became good citizens, some chose to leave and settled in the Canadian provinces of New Brunswick and Nova Scotia. Most of the men from the Carolinas remained near their homes, or they resettled in Florida or Europe. The man who formally surrendered the Loyalist Militia at King's Mountain, Capt. Abraham DePeyster, was held prisoner until the end of the war and eventually settled in Saint John, New Brunswick. He defended his actions at King's Mountain, although opportunistic accusations haunted him the remainder of his life. Yet, his men knew he did the right thing and defended his honor in the press, describing him as a "brave, good officer," and saying he "disputed the ground as long as it was possible to defend it." DePeyster rose to the rank of colonel in the provincial militia and he served as New Brunswick's provincial treasurer until he died in 1799.

Other Loyalists of note included Lt. Anthony Allaire, who also moved to New Brunswick and served under DePeyster in the provincial militia. Allaire died in 1838. Ferguson's Loyalist adjutant, Alexander Chesney, was offered his freedom in return for service in the Patriot cause. Chesney refused, and he escaped from captivity, joined Tarleton's dragoons, and fought (and lost) again at the Battle of Cowpens. Patriot leader Daniel Morgan pursued Chesney, but he escaped and ultimately returned to his native Ireland. After the war, Chesney continued to insist that Ferguson himself fired the shots that killed Colonel Williams, but we will never know for certain. The lone surgeon of King's Mountain, Dr. Uzal Johnson, returned to his home in Newark, New Jersey, after the war. Johnson continued his devotion to the practice of medicine until he died on May 22, 1827.

The final individual of note is Capt. William Green, whose strange story highlights the ideological differences, the confusing times, and the emotional drama that brought the combatants together at the battle of King's Mountain. Green was born and raised in the shadow of King's Mountain along the boundary of the two Carolinas. When the war began he joined the Patriot cause, where he rose to the rank of captain. In 1780, when the British invaded the

Carolinas, Green turned his back to the Patriot cause and joined the Loyalists. Thus, at the Battle of King's Mountain, Green served as a captain under Major Ferguson, then became a prisoner in the hands of his former friends. After the battle, he was tried and condemned as a traitor, but he escaped. To atone his sins, Green rejoined the Patriots, where he served heroically until the end of the war. After the war, Green was elected to the North Carolina House of Commons and served fourteen terms in the State Senate. Green died in Rutherford County, North Carolina, on November 16, 1832.

Touring the Field

Overmountain Victory National Historic Trail

The route followed by the Overmountain Patriots has been designated by the National Park System as the "Overmountain Victory National Historic Trail" (OVNHT). Route maps are available from the National Park Service (ordered via mail or Internet or visit the King's Mountain National Park Visitor Center). The route can be traversed by vehicle on modern roads; however, each year the Overmountain Victory Trail Association conducts a road and hike reenactment to commemorate the trek to King's Mountain led in 1780 by Col. William Campbell. The route begins here in Abingdon, Virginia, at Dunn's Meadows.

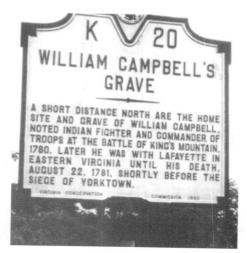

Historic site marker for William Campbell's grave

Historic markers are posted along the route and key points provide informational markers. Dunn's Meadows was the designated muster point for the Washington County militia on September 23, 1780, and was certified by the National Park Service on September 24, 1999, as the starting point of the Overmountain Victory National Historic Trail. The site is on private property (the Dunn family) at 702 Colonial Road in Abingdon, Virginia. Abingdon is a beautiful town steeped in history and filled with wonderful historic sites of the Revolution and the Civil War era. Nearby in the community of Seven Mile Ford is the gravesite of Col. William Campbell, at his old homestead on State Route 642 in Aspenvale. His grave is clearly marked with a large tombstone and a commemorative state marker.

The OVNHT winds through the Holston River Valley along a beautiful rural route through Washington County. Looming parallel along the southeast side of the road is the Iron Mountain range (part of the Blue Ridge Mountains). The OVNHT follows U.S. 11 east to Virginia 75, then it traverses southward, crossing the Tennessee line where Virginia 75 becomes Tennessee 44. Follow Tennessee 44 south to U.S. 421.

Campbell's militiamen made their first stop at a militia rally point known to locals as the Pemberton Oak. This large tree still stands today and is estimated to be 700 years old (it has been used as a rally point in several wars throughout our nation's history). At this rally point, Campbell's force was strengthened by men under the command of Capt. John Pemberton. From here, the OVNHT proceeds north on U.S. 421 to Bristol, Tennessee. In Bristol, turn left on State Street and continue to U.S. 11/19. Today, Bristol Virginia-Tennessee is a thriving modern city, yet it honors its rich southern heritage with a variety of historical and cultural events and museums.

Col. Isaac Shelby's forces traveled southeastward also from their fort at Sapling Grove (now known as Bristol,

The Pemberton Oak, the seven-hundred-year-old oak, where Colonel William Campbell's men assembled for their march to Sycamore Shoals.

Tennessee). Go south until U.S. 19E turns left toward Elizabethton. Follow U.S. 19E south to U.S. 321 toward Elizabethton and turn left into the Sycamore Shoals State Historic Site.

The state park at Sycamore Shoals includes a recreated version of Fort Watauga, the initial gathering site for the muster of the "Overmountain Men," with palisades and blockhouses, as well as a museum with original artifacts of the period. The site offers excellent interpretive displays, a bookstore, park guides, and beautiful scenery. The site is on the original location on the Watauga River, which winds along the base of the Blue Ridge Mountains. The town of Elizabethton is a modern, hospitable town complete with motels and restaurants. Continue traveling along the OVNHT by turning left on U.S. 321 to Gap Creek Road in Elizabethton, Tennessee. Turn left and follow Gap Creek Road south past the junction with Tennessee and continue south to U.S. 19E. Turn right and follow U.S. 19E south to the North Carolina line. Enjoy the beautiful drive and imagine the frigid trek as experienced by the Overmountain Men in these elevations.

Fort Watauga at Sycamore Shoals

Continuing along the OVNHT, travel southward on U.S. 19E in North Carolina through Avery County to Spruce Pine. Here the OVNHT turns left onto North Carolina 226. Follow N.C. 226 east across the Blue Ridge Parkway into Marion. Go east on U.S. 70 toward Morganton. Turn left onto North Carolina 126 toward Morganton.

Turn right onto North Carolina 181 and proceed eastward, joining with U.S. 64 at Sanford Drive. From Morganton, follow U.S. 64 west (Victory Trail) to Rutherfordton. Just before reaching Rutherfordton you will see the historic marker that designates the whereabouts of the old community known as Gilbert. Continuing on to Rutherfordton, turn left on U.S. 221 south past the courthouse to North Carolina 108. Turn right and then left immediately thereafter (be careful). Follow N.C. 108 past the Rutherfordton Elementary School and the hospital. Continue on N.C. 108 south towards Columbus and Tryon. At Mill Springs, turn left on N.C. 9 and proceed south. At the fork. proceed to the left towards Chesnee, leaving N.C. 9 (which continues to Spartanburg, S.C.).

Now the OVNHT makes a series of confusing turns, but they follow the original route of the Overmountain Men. From N.C. 9, follow a series of road changes that form a continuous route toward South Carolina 11: N.C. 1343, N.C. 1102, S.C. 58, S.C. 73. At S.C. 11, turn left and proceed east toward Chesnee. At the water tower just outside Chesnee, turn left on Tank Road (S.C. 101 and S.C. 146) and continue through a residential area and carefully across U.S. 221 to S.C. 144. Turn left on S.C. 146 and continue to a dead end at S.C. 11. Turn left on S.C. 11 and continue east past the Cowpens National Battlefield towards Gaffney. While you are in this area you should visit the Cowpens National Battlefield Park to see where the Patriots defeated Tarleton's dragoons on January 17, 1781.

The OVNHT crosses Interstate 85, then turns left into North Carolina 18. When N.C. 18 turns left to re-cross Interstate 85, continue straight ahead on South Carolina 329 to U.S. 29. Turn left and follow U.S. 29 north to South Carolina 30. Turn right and follow S.C. 30 until the trail turns into South Carolina 207 and continue along this route.

Continuing travel on the OVNHT, South Carolina 207 passes Cherokee Ford (where the Mountain Men crossed the Broad River) back to S.C. 30. Turn right and continue to South Carolina 5. Turn right and follow S.C. 5 to South Carolina 66. Turn left and follow S.C. 66 to South Carolina 21. These rural roads wound through this area as a trail in colonial days.

Continuing along the OVNHT on South Carolina 21, turn right and go past the Antioch Baptist Church to the junction with South Carolina 216. Go right and follow S.C. 216 into King's Mountain National Military Park. Just as you enter the park on S.C. 216, a large ravine below the immediate high ground to your front concealed the Overmountain Men as they planned their attack of Ferguson's Tory forces on King's Mountain. The battlefield can be seen on the dominant terrain in the distance. The OVNHT on S.C. 216 winds on around the mountain for a short distance, where you turn left into the battlefield's museum and visitors' center.

VISITING THE BATTLEFIELD

King's Mountain National Military Park was established on March 3, 1931, "in order to commemorate the Battle of King's Mountain." The park is located just south of Interstate 85 about thirty-five miles between the metropolitan cities of Charlotte, North Carolina, and Greenville, South Carolina. Major airlines, rental cars, hotels and restaurants are available in either city. From Greenville, South Carolina, travel on I-85 north to North Carolina Exit 2. From Charlotte, North Carolina, travel on I-85 south to North Carolina Exit 2. As you exit the interstate from either direction, you will turn onto Highway 216 South and you are now within a five-minute drive from the battlefield park. Just after you enter Highway 216, you cross the state border into South Carolina. Both Patriot and British forces approached King's Mountain along this road, although in October of 1780 it was a muddy, wagon-rutted colonial trail. Shortly after you cross King's Creek, you ascend the slope of the King's Mountain range and enter King's Mountain National Military Park. The sixteen-mile range before you extends from the left (northeast) in North Carolina and stretches across to your right (southwest) through South Carolina. The upper or northeast end of the range contains the highest elevations, while in the vicinity of the battlefield, the average elevation is 1,000 feet. The road curves southward through the forest as you pass the park administration office on your right. You are now within one mile of your destination and in the woods to your left, upon the heights, is the King's Mountain battlefield. However, you will continue winding on around the mountain and turn left into the visitor center parking lot. Call ahead for hours, but the park is typically open daily, 9 A.M. to 5 P.M.; weekends, 9 A.M. to 6 P.M. (Memorial Day to Labor Day) and closed on Thanksgiving Day, Christmas Day, and New Year's Day. The visitor center is a modern, spacious facility and the entire battlefield is handicap accessible.

While inside the visitor center be sure to watch the eighteen-minute film, *King's Mountain: Turning Point in the South*, which provides an excellent overview of the battle. A small museum exhibits weapons, uniforms, and equipment used by the combatants. In the main lobby, there is also a good Eastern National bookstore that sells literature focused on the American Revolution, several narratives of the battle, and maps and gift items. Before leaving the visitor center, obtain a battlefield brochure and tour map, which will greatly enhance your visit. Directly behind the center is a one-and-a-half–mile self-guiding trail that loops its way around the battlefield. The trail is handicap-capable and a wheelchair is available at the visitor center. While the route is evenly paved, six feet wide and easily traversed, it is steep in various areas; thus assistance is advisable for anyone using a wheelchair.

The trail winds its way around the base of the mountain, which the Patriots encircled. The trail then loops around and traverses the length of the ridge, which the Loyalists attempted to defend. Along the trail key points concerning the battle are highlighted through graphic displays, monuments, and wayside exhibits. Highlights include Ferguson's Cairn, the burial site of British Maj. Patrick Ferguson, the U.S. Memorial Monument, and graphic exhibits of key events. As a pleasant addition to the history lesson, the hike through the Carolina woods also provides a presentation of the flora and fauna. A minimum of three hours is recommended to view the exhibits and hike the battlefield trail. Winters are mild, with the lowest temperatures generally in the twenties. Summers are hot and humid with high temperatures in the nineties. Late fall and early spring provide optimum viewing of the battlefield terrain.

King's Mountain National Military Park and the adjoining King's Mountain State Park have combined efforts to offer sixteen miles of hiking trails and over sixteen miles of horse trails. There is one isolated campsite near the battlefield at Garner Creek, three miles from the visitor center. Availability is first-come, first-served. Register at the visitor center the day you want to camp. Additional camp-sites are available in the adjoining state park, which has a 116-site campground open year-round. It too operates on a first-come basis. Additional information about the campground is available by calling (803) 222–3209. The park operates a small store that sells food and supplies. Picnicking and camping facilities are provided year-round and seasonal activities include swimming and miniature golf. The state park also offers programs at a reconstructed eighteenth-century farm. Restaurants, lodging, and fuel are available nearby in King's Mountain and Gastonia, North Carolina, as well as Gaffney and Blacksburg, South Carolina.

The battlefield park also serves as the terminus of the Overmountain Victory National Historic Trail, which com-memorates the route taken by the Patriot army from the mountains to the battle. Each fall, reenactors in frontier clothing assemble across the Blue Ridge Mountains in Virginia and Tennessee, then retrace the 220-mile route to King's Mountain. The annual event marks the anniversary of the battle and honors the heroes of King's Mountain. It also animates our American history and provides a unique educational experience for all ages.

Visitors should note that twenty-eight miles southwest is Cowpens National Battlefield, where the Patriot army camped the night before the battle of King's Mountain. Additionally, in 1781, it was also the scene of a battle where Patriot forces commanded by General Daniel Morgan defeated the infamous British dragoon, Lt. Col. Banastre Tarleton.

Additional information can be obtained from:
King's Mountain National Military Park
2625 Park Road
Blacksburg, S.C. 29702
(864) 936-7921
FAX: (864) 936-9897

Battlefield Photo Tour

Major Hambright's line of attack from the east

Major Joseph Winston's line of attack from the southeast

Patriot assault lines along the eastern slope of King's Mountain

Patriot assault lines looking from the north and east toward
British positions on King's Mountain

Major William Chronicle's line of attack from the northeast and his memorial marker at the location of his death

Another view of Chronicle's line of attack

Patriot assault lines looking from the north. Colonel Cleveland's extreme left tied in with Chronicle's right.

Patriot assault lines along the northern base of King's Mountain

Natural spring located between Williams's and Shelby's lines

Shelby's assault line looking toward the southeast

Sevier's forces attacked up the western slope of the mountain. This view is looking north along the battlefield trail.

View looking south, showing Sevier's line of attack. British forces occupied the heights at the upper left of the photo.

British position at the extreme western end of King's Mountain. The view is looking west and down toward Sevier's assault lines.

British defenders extended from here to the northeast along the ridge. Patriot assault lines came in from the west and south.

Looking west from British positions atop King's Mountain. Sevier's men assaulted directly into this sector, while Campbell attacked from the left (south).

Erected at the highest point on King's Mountain (1020 feet), the Centennial Monument honors the Patriot Americans who fought here.

Looking down the trail along the ridgeline from the Centennial Monument. Patriot units mingled after British bayonet charges.

Marker honoring Colonel Asbury Coward

Looking down the trail along the ridgeline. As British units retreated to the northeast side of the ridge, they were forced into an ever-shrinking enclave.

Reverse angle view of above, now looking northeast to southwest. Sevier, Shelby, and Campbell's men pressed the British from the north, south, and west.

Monument erected by the U.S. government in honor of all the men who fought in the Battle of King's Mountain

McDowell

Williams

View of the U.S. monument looking from the northeast to the southwest

Marker honoring Colonel James Hawthorn

Looking down the trail along the ridgeline, from the southwest to the northeast—the direction of the British retreat

Marker designating the location where the commander of British forces, Major Patrick Ferguson, was mortally wounded

Just below and north of the Ferguson marker is another marker honoring Colonel Frederick Hambright who was wounded here in battle.

Looking down and south of the Ferguson marker at the top of the ridge, you can see the area where Ferguson was buried.

View looking uphill toward the marker designating the location where Ferguson fell in battle

Looking downhill toward Ferguson's grave

Looking uphill from Ferguson's grave

Ferguson's cairn and memorial marker

View from Major Joseph Winston's assault line in the southeast
sector of King's Mountain.

SUGGESTED READINGS

Original historical records of Loyalists and Patriots who served on King's Mountain are rare, and the starting point for serious research is the Lyman C. Draper manuscripts. These records are vast, but not widely available. There is a microfilm copy (twelve rolls) available in the King's Mountain National Military Park Archives (you must request an appointment through the park director). These manuscripts consist of the personal collections of the chief chronicler of King's Mountain and they span several decades of letters and notes. Draper used his manuscripts to write the definitive book on the topic, *King's Mountain and Its Heroes*, published in 1881. The book has been reprinted and is readily available today. Several other books that use the Draper manuscripts as well as very rare British records are the rosters of the participants at King's Mountain, edited and compiled by historian Dr. Bobby Moss. These rosters provide excellent references that list details concerning the individual contributions of both the Patriots and Loyalists who fought at King's Mountain. *The Loyalists at King's Mountain* is exceptionally valuable to anyone studying the membership of that greatly overlooked element of the Revolutionary War. This book uses a compilation of rare British and American documents that define the membership of the Tory participants. Likewise, Dr. Moss has compiled the Patriot roster, entitled *The Patriots at King's Mountain*. Other recommended sources that provide additional information about this battle are listed below.

Allaire, Anthony. *Diary of Lieutenant Anthony Alliare.* New York: Arno, 1968; original publication, 1881.

Braisted, Todd, et al. *The On-Line Institute for Advanced Loyalist Studies.* Unpublished manuscripts and notes concerning the Loyalist Militia. Some material is available via the Internet: http://www.royalprovincial.com/index.htm .

Chidsey, Donald B. *The War in the South: The Carolinas and Georgia in the American Revolution.* New York: Crown, 1969.

Clinton, Henry. *The American Rebellion: Sir Henry Clinton's Narrative.* New Haven: Yale University, 1954.

Crow, Jeffrey J., and Larry E. Tise. *The Southern Experience in the American Revolution.* Chapel Hill: University of North Carolina, 1978.

DePeyster, J. Watts. "The Affair at King's Mountain." *Magazine of American History* 5 (December 1880): pp. 401–424.

Draper, Lyman C. *King's Mountain and its Heroes: History of the Battle of King's Mountain, October 7, 1780, and the Events Which Led to it.* Cincinnati, Ohio: Thompson, 1881. Also 1996 reprint, The Overmountain Press.

Drayton, John. *Memoirs of the American Revolution as Relating to the State of South Carolina,* two volumes. New York: Arno, 1969; original publication, 1821.

Ervin, Sara S. *South Carolinians in the Revolution.* Baltimore: Genealogical, 1981.

Gibbs, R. W., ed. *Documentary History of the American Revolution: Consisting of Letters and Papers Relating to the Contest for Liberty, Chiefly in South Carolina.* Three volumes. New York: Appleton, 1855.

Hilborn, Nat and Sam. *Battleground of Freedom: South Carolina in the Revolution.* Columbia, S.C.: Sandlapper, 1970.

Mackenzie, George C. *Kings Mountain National Military Park, South Carolina.* National Park Service Historical Handbook No. 22, 1955.

Mackenzie, Roderick. *Strictures on Lt. Col. Tarleton's History of the Campaigns of 1780 and 1781, in the Southern Province of North America.* London: Mackenzie, 1787.

McGrady, Edward. *The History of South Carolina in the Revolution, 1775–1783*. Two volumes. New York: Macmillan, 1901–1902.

Messick, Hank. *King's Mountain: The Epic of the Blue Ridge "Mountain Men" in the American Revolution*. Boston: Little Brown, 1976.

Moss, Bobby Gilmer. *Diary of a Loyalist Surgeon: Uzal Johnson*. Blacksburg, S.C.: Scotia-Hibernia Press, 2000.

_____. *The Loyalist at King's Mountain*. Blacksburg, S.C.: Scotia-Hibernia Press, 1998.

_____. *The Patriots at King's Mountain*. Blacksburg, S.C.: Scotia Press, 1990.

Schenck, David. *North Carolina, 1780–81: Being a History of the Invasion of the Carolinas by the British Army under Lord Cornwallis in 1780–81*. Raleigh, N.C.: Edwards and Broughton, 1889. Also 1967 reprint.

Skaggs, David C. "Kings Mountain and the Denouement of Southern Loyalism." *Military Review* 55 (April 1975): pp. 56–60.

Tarleton, Banastre. *A History of the Campaigns of 1780 and 1781, in the Southern Provinces of North America*. London: Cadell, 1787.

U.S. Army War College. Historical Section. *Historical Statements Concerning the Battle of King's Mountain and the Battle of Cowpens South Carolina*. House Doc. No. 328, 70th Congress, 1928.

U.S. President (Hoover). *Address of President Hoover on the Occasion of the Celebration of the One Hundred and Fiftieth Anniversary of the Battle of King's Mountain*. Washington, D.C.: Government Printing Office, 1930.

Weigley, Russell F. *The Partisan War: The South Carolina Campaign of 1780–1782*. Columbia, S.C.: University of South Carolina, 1970.

INDEX

Index